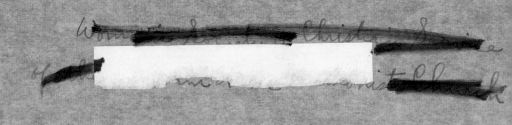

Woman's Society of Christian Service
of the ~~ Methodist Church~~

THE WILL
TO
BELIEVE

THE WILL
TO
BELIEVE

by

MARCUS BACH

Englewood Cliffs, N.J.
PRENTICE-HALL, INC.

PRINTED IN THE UNITED STATES OF AMERICA

96015

To
Lorena

I asked them, "What do you have that I lack?"
Their answer was always the same:

> *The Will to Believe.*

Then I found it.

Soon others were asking me, "What do you have that I lack?"
My answer was always the same:

> *The Will to Believe.*

Contents

PART I

THE WILL TO BELIEVE
IN THE WORLD AND
THE LIFE WITHIN

CONTENTS

PART II

THE WILL TO BELIEVE
IN THE WORLD AND
THE LIFE AROUND

CONTENTS

PART III

THE WILL TO BELIEVE IN THE WORLD AND THE LIFE BEYOND

CONTENTS

THE WILL
TO
BELIEVE

Part I

THE WILL TO BELIEVE
IN THE WORLD
AND
THE LIFE WITHIN

1. The World Is Built on the Will to Believe

The most important and the most unnoticed quality in the world is the will to believe. It plays its part every time we drop a letter in a postal box or board a plane or do the thousand-and-one routine things that make up our modern life. From the money we bank to the money we borrow, from our hope for a better future to the conviction that yesterday was not without meaning, from accepting the universe to rejecting a weather report, we live in a world built on faith.

The Most Important Quality

This is hardly a new idea. What *is* new is a greater awakening to the fact that the greater the will to believe, the greater and richer your life.

5

For a long while now, we have been caught in a rash of books on how to be a success, how to win friends, how to make good, how to be popular, how to make money, how to spend it, and how to live to be a hundred. However, one thing has been consistently overlooked by authors and consistently looked for by readers: the secret of coming to terms with life according to one's own innermost nature.

Certainly there are plenty of us who don't aspire to live to be a hundred, don't envy the man with a million, and have no desire to pay the penalty for being popular. What we want is the formula for being ourselves, not someone else. What we are interested in is living according to the nature that is distinctively our own, rather than being made over into some other ego. And we aren't ready to admit that we are pathological because we want to be what we honestly feel we *are*.

A Specific Purpose for Your Own Special Life

By the way, what *has* happened to our individualism? Why must we all suddenly be stereotyped and famous and successful and so well-adjusted that we can be counted off as statistics in a public poll? Where would this old world be if it were not for individuals who insisted on being themselves? What would life be like if it weren't for the nonconformists?

Thank the Lord for the "heretics": a Jesus who laid

down His life to fulfill the promise of God's love for men; a Ghandi who found God in discipline; a Schweitzer who found Him in human service.

Thank the Lord for the "fanatics": a Francis of Assisi who talked with the birds; a George Fox who communed with an inner voice; a William Blake who had visions and dreams.

Thank the Lord for the "iconoclasts" of many faiths: a Jew like Haym Salomon who gave his fortune for the cause of American liberty; a Catholic like Lord Baltimore who blueprinted a text for freedom of worship; a Protestant like William Penn who practiced it.

Thank the Lord for the "madmen" of many races: a George Washington Carver who saw no conflict between religion and science; a Kagawa who recognized no barrier between religion and education; a Kahlil Gibran who found no disagreement between religion and life.

These men lived greatly and adventurously because each had a will to believe in a specific purpose for his own particular life. Each considered himself an individual expression, an original creation, and refused to be boiled down, stirred up, and molded into a fixed and standardized form. Each lived his own life and therefore each lives on, and we live better because of them.

There Is No One Quite Like You in the World

You are a distinctive and individual expression of a

7

Creative Force. You are not a blueprint or a carbon copy or a ditto of anyone past, present or future. You are *you* and there is no one quite like you in the world.

You don't look exactly like anyone else, you don't think exactly like anyone else, you don't live exactly like anyone else. There are things you can do better than anyone else can do them, and there are qualities and talents that no one else possesses in exactly the same way that you do. There are thoughts that are your own special revelation. That which makes you YOU is personal, unique and exclusive. All of this is a reflection of a world and a life *within*.

Talk about how to be a success! The successful person is simply the one who does his best with the things he can do better than anyone else.

Talk about living well! Who lives better than the one who is true to his own inner light?

Talk about being interesting! Who is more interesting than the person who is being himself?

Talk about how to be happy! The happy, self-unfolded people are those who, with a will to believe in the world and the life within, have found that the secret of really getting the most out of life is to make the most of the qualities that are innately their own.

Your Individuality Is Your Greatest Heritage

We find these people everywhere: a farm girl who

8

discovers she can write children's stories; a grandmother who realizes she is an artist; a man in a lonely mountain cabin who finds his talent is tying trout flies; a housewife whose "life within" happens to be rich in the field of musical therapy; a man who whittles just for the sake of whittling; a fellow who calls square dances for the sheer joy of calling square dances; a mathematical genius or a man who adds up figures at a high desk in a midwestern grain elevator; a linguist or a fellow who knows only a hillbilly brogue; a photographer for *Life* or for the hometown weekly; a cook at the Waldorf or over a kitchen stove; an architect or the carpenter; a teacher or the student; the man in the front office or the laborer on the assembly line; everywhere, from the occupant of a country shack to the owner of a country estate—for every individual there is a *world within* that is inviolately his own.

You cannot socialize this away from a man. You cannot rob him of it or absorb this into any communal experiment. You may dictate what a man should read or not read, you may prescribe how he should act or not act, you may legislate and regulate his public life, but you will never take from him what he *wills to believe* about himself. His philosophy, his ideas of right and wrong, his opinions, his relationship with God and the unknown; these are *his* and no man or group of men can ever divest him of this, his own secret inner world. And this world is yours.

9

What Is in Each of Us That Makes Us Great?

This inner world grows as we will to believe in it. It is not through searching or feverish groping that we enter into it. It is through the gateway of our will to believe. You will to believe that because you are an individual expression of God, there is purpose, real and meaningful, in your life, and you will to believe that to achieve this purpose you are also equipped with the talent and potential necessary for its achievement. Will to believe it!

There is that within each of us that makes us great— I do not mean greatness in the sense of getting one's name in the headlines or making a million, but greatness in the sense of coming to terms with God and life. We might call it getting hold of a guiding principle and making life count in terms of what we are and have and want to be. For it is the originality in each of us and not our uniformity which gives life its deepest meaning.

In this world within, your world, you are the most important figure. There is a place that no one else can fill. There is an influence that no one else can impart. There is a life that no one can live quite as well as you can live it. What you do with your life within, in terms of self-realization, self-awareness, self-denial and self-expression, is the greatest challenge that can come to you.

10

There Is a Law

The will to believe in a world and a life within extends much further than the recognition of a distinctively inner life and inner light. Your will to believe is based not only on a greatness within but also on a law within. It is an immutable law, a law of causality, a law of the relation of cause and effect.

This law of causality is operative within the universe. You can depend upon the stars. You can argue strongly for a God of reason and right as you observe the cosmos.

This law of causality is also operative within nature. You can depend on like begetting like. There are those who maintain that since nature's laws are mathematically dependable, that is how God must be.

But what about the moral argument? Are we ready to say that an immutable law is also at work within the life of man? Can this be proved? Can you prove unmistakably that if you are friendly, others will be friendly to you? That if you plant kindness, you will reap kindness? Can you prove that if you think health you will be healthy, and if you think sickness you will be sick; that if you give you will be given unto, and that if you steal you will be stolen from?

Can you prove that if you do good you will get good breaks and if you do evil you will get bad breaks? Is your present lot in life what you have merited? Does

11

your life *prove* the result of some divine law, some immense karmic cycle, some cause and effect, some unalterable process that can be depended upon and measured and worked with and perhaps even be dimly understood?

In short, are you prepared to say that "as a man sows, so shall he reap?" There is surely evidence of such a law, but if you wait until you can prove it you will be a long time waiting. *Will to believe it!* And in your believability you will remake and improve your world. "Oh God," cried Leonardo da Vinci, "you sell us everything for the price of an effort!"

Saving Yourself From Doubt

There is a good chance that somewhere along the way you have been trapped by doubt about the dependability of this world and this life within.

There is, for example, the time of intellectual crisis, when all of a sudden reality does not seem to line up with religious idealism. There is also the time of academic conflict, when dogmatism is found to be incompatible with science, as indeed dogmatism and science must ever be.

Or there may be the moment of agonizing disillusionment, when religion as a deeply personal experience is shipwrecked in the muddy theological waters, or when some social situation involving the misdeeds of trusted

12

friends jars your faith. There is also the fearful sense of frustration when we feel that we ourselves would want to be kinder than God seems to be to us. And there is, above all, the sense of loss when we look out across the world and feel there is no rhyme or reason behind the fate of men or nations. Yes, there is a good possibility that somewhere along the way, doubt as to the rightness of the world and the life within will ambush every one of us.

In all of this there is but one sure and stabilizing force. We must exercise a *will to believe,* and by an act of faith determine that for us God *is* just and Heaven *is* kind, and that there *is* an immutable law operative in all of life. To believe this and to live according to this belief requires effort and work. You see, we have had the mistaken idea that faith comes easily, that it is a free gift. The individualist knows better. The honest searcher knows better. Every one who has ever tried to live according to his highest ideals knows better.

We stand in constant danger of losing our faith because we will not make the effort to save it from being engulfed by doubt. We want proof, but what we need is a will to believe. We must consciously overcome wrong thinking, wrong propaganda, a wrong sense of values, in order to get the most out of life.

"The soul is the light of man," sang the Hindu sages.

"As a man thinketh in his heart, so is he," wrote Solomon.

13

"The superior man is quiet, waiting for the appointments of heaven," remarked Confucius.

"Know thyself," said the Oracle to Socrates.

"The Kingdom of Heaven is within you!" said Jesus.

Keep Your Spiritual Shoulders Back

Recently I met an elderly man who had amazed a TV audience with his poise and youthful outlook on life. When I asked whether he had any special secret to live by, he said, "Early in life I learned to keep my shoulders back. Whenever I consciously did that, I felt better, I thought better, I walked straighter, and lived straighter."

"Was it easy to do this?" I asked.

"It has always been a fight to keep those shoulders back," he told me.

What this man accomplished in walking straight, others have achieved in thinking straight and living straight. And, of course, there is a relation between the two practices. There is also a relation in the fact that something in us tries to keep us from being straight. The sleeping giant of self-realization, the inner man, our *true self*, needs the help of a conscious effort.

Do not let adverse circumstances and thoughts of defeat mislead you. They are the common lot of every thinking person. Triumph over them with a will to believe that the Kingdom of God, the real worth of

14

life, the true value of things, lies in the awareness that every moment is alive with the presence of an inner power.

Life for free men is always a struggle; that is why they are free. Faith works only where we work at our faith; these are words the churches ought to write above their altars so that every complacent worshiper might see them. Faith works only where we work at our faith. The will to believe in a world and a life within requires effort.

What Can a Man Honestly Believe?

A graduate student with understandable anguish came into my office. The previous day his only child had burned to death in her crib while the mother was momentarily out of the apartment. A stove had exploded and caused the tragedy.

The student put his concern to me bluntly, "Why did this happen to my child? What can religion do for me now?"

Some religionists would have had an answer. They would have told him that this awful happening must have been retribution for some secret sin of which the student or his wife had been guilty. The mills of God . . . the omnipotent and relentless judgment of God . . . heaven's retaliatory power. . . . This, they would contend, was the law of causality, stark and clear.

15

Others would have attested with equal sincerity and less bitterness that inasmuch as something was wrong with the stove and that since the child and the crib were situated as they were, it was just "one of those things." Yes, they would say, it was the working of an immutable law, if that's what you want to call it. The gas accumulated, the gas exploded, the child was killed.

A third might have explained it this way, "It is part of a karmic cycle. There is a meaning here, though not clear perhaps, which is unalterably related with previous existences and existences yet to be."

Each would have had an answer and an explanation. I didn't. I said to the student, "I don't know why this happened to you. More than that, I don't know why it should happen to any parent. I don't understand unexpected tragedy any more than I do unexpected triumph. It is as difficult for me to explain a misfortune that is entirely between an innocent child and God as it is for me to explain a 'miracle' between an innocent child and God. I just don't know. But in answer to your question as to what religion can do for you, I can tell you this: religion and only religion can provide you with a will to believe at that point where reason stands confounded."

"A will to believe in what?"

"In a world and a life within, and in the truth that this world and this life within is God in you, so that everything that happens to you reveals God more clearly. Deep within our knowing is a greater knowing. What-

16

ever my conception of that knowing is, whatever my views or definition of God may be, I know that mine is merely one of many thousands of equally sincere concepts. But I know that every honest concept is based on a will to believe that God is good despite any feeling and question and opinion we may have to the contrary.

"It is that way with suffering. I have never learned the reason for suffering, but I know that whatever conclusion I come to, mine is only one of thousands of equally honest views about it. And every honest view is based on a will to believe that suffering leaves one strengthened and refined. What we all desperately need, and heaven knows it is not easy, is to trust where we cannot see, and to walk in faith where reason refuses to be our guide. To everyone who has this will to believe there comes a day when he can once more honestly trust and fearlessly walk with understanding."

2. How You Can Come to Terms with Life

I REMEMBER THE DAY WHEN THOUGHTS about a will to believe became crystal-clear. It was on the occasion of a visit with my mother in a nursing home in a little Wisconsin town. She was in her seventies, a recent stroke having left her partially paralyzed and much changed from the mother I had known.

She had been one of the most devoted religious workers, churchwise, that any congregation could possibly have had. She had baked more meat-loaf for the glory of God than any woman in Protestantism. This should also apply to angel food cakes! She had been secretary of the church consistory, a member of the Indian Mission Board, president of the Ladies' Aid, and for fifty years a teacher in the Sunday School, and she had entertained and fed more preachers in our home than was good for either the preachers or her.

And every Sunday, come rain or snow or summer sun,

21

mother would be in the third pew front in the old church surrounded by her brood of kids. When we had all left home, one by one, she sat there with Dad. And when Dad died, she sat there alone, listening to sermons as if they were always new, joining in the ritual as if it could never lose its charm, and praying as if God would be glad to know that she was still there in her selfsame place.

Now, confronted by the tumbling altars of her little world, she spoke to me despairingly as I sat at her bedside.

"Look at me," she said. "What do you make of all this? I tell you, when I look back upon life and religion, I begin to have questions about God and the meaning of it all. Things have even gone better with the Free-thinkers who never went to church than they have with me. What is a person to say?"

It was a good question. I could have recommended a whole library of books which show that ever since the first faltering search for meaning behind the universe, men have tried to find the answer to dilemmas just like hers. The primitive savage and the modern scientist stand here on an equal footing: can the Unknown ever be found out? Neither the savage nor the scientist has ever solved man's ways, let alone the ways of God.

How I Learned Life's Greatest Lesson

Perhaps I should have turned her problem over to an

22

epistemologist or an ontologist or a theologian or a psychiatrist. Or perhaps discussed at length the whole ideology of the Christian faith, beginning with the Christianity of Christ, to the Christianity of the Apostolic Church, the Christianity of her day and my day, and the Christianity of the world with the "bottom dropped out," as someone once said. I should at least have set her right about her "sense of values" and reminded her of all she still had for which to be thankful.

I had only one reply. There was just one thing I could say with all the honesty of my heart and out of the discoveries of my years of research.

I said, "You know, Mother, that's just the way it looks to me, too. You of all people should have had some happy final years. You are the one person whom I would have considered supremely worthy of all the good that God could possibly give. I remember how you always dreamed that you would have a little home of your own in which, without being a burden to anyone, you could spend these years of your life. I remember how you had visions of going back to see your native Switzerland and how you had set your heart on that. I know how you feel and why you have asked me what you have. I agree with you. Sometimes there doesn't seem to be any rhyme or reason in the universe, and the old law of cause and effect seems certainly to have snapped."

She looked at me dully, trying to comprehend my words. Then her eyes filled with surprise and pain.

23

"I didn't expect you to talk like that," she ventured.

"Why not?" I answered. "Don't you think every thinking person has his moments of doubts and questioning?"

She looked at me as if I were daring to put into words a closely-guarded secret.

"But what do you think we should do?" I asked. "Shall we take our place over here with those who say, 'God is fickle, God is unjust, God plays His favorites— He has finally let me down?' Or shall we stand over here with those who insist that, 'God is not fickle. God is just; He shows no favoritism. Even though I do not understand, even though I see through a glass darkly, I will not deny Him.' You know, there was a man who in the moment of his greatest tragedy, which was perhaps the moment of his greatest triumph, said, 'Even though He slay me, yet will I trust Him.' Where do you think someone like you or I should stand?"

Her hand was already reaching for mine. There was no question about what she thought, or about what I was thinking. That feeling, that conviction, that assurance was built on just one thing: a will to believe. We could prove nothing. We could explain nothing. We stood on the narrow, razor-like edge of a hypothetical case, and we threw the weight of our belief against the weight of unbelief to keep us walking straight and firm with the highest idealism of which we felt ourselves capable.

24

For surely we become like the things in which we believe. Our thoughts make us what we are. We take on the characteristics of our convictions. The moment we will to believe that God is just, in that moment we become more just in our outlook and our life. And if we believe in the sanctity of the world and the life within, we shall certainly ascribe to God, the Giver of life, a higher sanctity than that of which we ourselves are capable.

Here Is How You Can Understand Life

You see, we have tried all too long to find proof of God's presence. We have struggled all too hard to find evidence of the law of causality in life. We plant a good deed and it does not seem to grow; we sow a good thought and we cannot find the fruit we think it should yield. I repeat, it is not proof we need, it is faith; the kind of deep and holy faith that Jesus must have harbored even when He felt Himself forsaken.

Everything He talked about was directed toward the individual and the discovery of one's inner self. He had surprisingly little to say about world peace or world affairs or world conferences. The recurrent theme which He brought, the pulse-beat of His entire message, was this: you are a child of God . . . your body is the temple of the Holy Spirit . . . you are the person God needs.

So it was when He walked by the Galilean sea. So it

25

was when He called to those who worked there at their nets. He did not say, "Well, the world is in an awful state and there is nothing you can do about it." He saw within them the slumbering dynamic of great personal worth. He recognized that they had never realized their inner power. He knew what they needed and what the world needed—individuals awakened to their Godlikeness. What He wanted was to rouse them into believability concerning their own unique importance. In that moment, religion became to them a real and living force.

And That Is What Religion Is

It is a living force within *you*. It is a living response to the will to believe. It cannot be interpreted in terms of any one single tenet or creed. It includes the experiences on many paths, all of which lead to the same eternal goal. It is not an accumulation of facts, it is not theology, it is not even prayer. It is the distillation of all that life is and was and hopes to be. It is the interplay between God and you.

It insists that a person ought to do what is right simply for the sake of righteousness, and ought to be good for the plain joy of goodness. When this is understood and recognized, religion becomes a reaching out by means of a volitional act; without questions or questioning, without argumentation, without fear, without hope of

26

reward or desire for gain, it causes us to will to believe in the highest concept of which our will to believe is capable.

There is, then, a world and a life within you, built completely upon a will to believe, and it is in the working of this world and this life that you come nearest to an understanding of God in you. You cannot find God for someone else. You can only help another find his God within himself, and you cannot even do this if you have not first found God within yourself.

3. The Master Key to the Life Within

Our AWARENESS OF THE WORLD AND the life within is deepened through the use of religious techniques and spiritual exercises. Put relative judgment aside for the moment, think of every man in terms of his own individual capacity and need, and you will agree, I am sure, that there are desirable virtues and helpful aids in so-called holy habits.

How Life Becomes the Great Adventure

It does not matter whether these were suggested by saints of old or modern men of daring faith. When the 16th-century saint, Francis de Sales, said, "I want very little, and what I do want I have very little wish for," he was certainly not of the same opinion that the modern

31

founder of a mail-order religion was when he, Frank B. Robinson, proclaimed, "Your Father is rich in houses and lands. What He has for Himself, He has for His children as well. He wants you to have what is His."

There is surely an appeal to at least two types of minds here! But when we take another glance at these two widely divergent personalities, one who lived in self-imposed poverty and the other in an up-to-date modern house in Idaho, one who walked quietly with sandaled feet and the other who drove a Cadillac, we find also some similarities in the matter of their spiritual exercises.

Thoughts Make Your World

"When you are alone," St. Francis suggested, "ponder a little and consider the variety of consolations, but especially of tribulations, that the good suffer; and then with great humility approve, praise and love all this will. Consider this will in your own person, in all the good or ill that happens to you and may happen to you, excepting sin; then approve, praise and love all that, protesting that you will ever cherish, honour and adore that sovereign will, and submitting to God's pleasure and giving Him all who are yours, amongst whom am I. End in a great confidence in that will, that it will work all good for us and our happiness. When you have performed this exercise two or three times in this way, you can shorten it, vary it and arrange it, as you find best, for it should often be thrust into your heart as an inspiration."

Now listen to what the strictly modern religionist has to say. Frank B. Robinson often told me, "There is no greater communion with God than to walk alone or stand alone in the quiet. Walking or standing, listen and try to hear His voice. Sure as you're born, He will speak to you if you listen. Who can say what He will say to you? He speaks to every man in His own way. The trouble with us is, we do not take time to listen. At first it is not easy. You may be disappointed. You may say, 'What am I doing? Listening to my own subconscious?' Who knows what the subconscious is? It may be that this in itself is God's voice. All I know is that the more you listen the more God will speak. Try it and see. And when you hear that voice, ponder what it says and give yourself over to His will for you in your life."

Could it be that the "saint" and the "businessman" were aiming at the same thing, each in his own way and each in his own time: a will to believe in the world and the life within?

Certainly each was prescribing a spiritual technique, and you may read into them as much profundity or as much simple knowledge as you wish.

I believe you may choose either the sandaled path or the Cadillac and be true to your own inner voice. What

33

was right for St. Francis de Sales was not necessarily right for Frank B. Robinson, and what was right for Frank B. Robinson would not have been right for St. Francis de Sales.

It is, of course, superfluous to point out that sandals and gunny sacks would be as ill-suited to our times as Cadillacs and TV sets would have been to the times of St. Francis. Though we all hear the complaint that we are living too well and too fast and not at all like Jesus would live were He on earth today, I have yet to find any of the complainers taking the first step in forfeiting the things they so loudly condemn.

What we need to do is to make Jesus, as philosopher Gerald Heard once said, "A guide for our conduct rather than a test for our credulity."

Techniques for Richer, Fuller Living

Spiritual exercises, religious practices and holy habits are secret keys which unlock the world and the life within. They may lead one type of individual into a monastery and another into the mid-stream of life, and each may honestly be following the way of truth and faith.

I was amused when a friend told me that religion taught him how to answer the doorbell. He said he used to become terribly upset when someone called at an inopportune time. Then he got hold of a technique;

rather, he got hold of an affirmation. Whenever the doorbell sounded or there was a disturbing knock just when he was settling down to work or rest, he would repeat to himself these words: "I go to meet my good!"

How did he know he was going to meet his good? He didn't know. He was inducing a will to believe that no one came to him unless the Father had sent him. Oh, so he was deceiving himself? No, he simply believed that the world and the life within were a link in a chain of divine providence in which everything that happened had meaning and purpose. He went on to tell me that it was unbelievable what interest he now found in people, and how often a visit which he would previously have shunned now took on new and profitable meaning. It's a technique. Easy? No. It is difficult. It requires a volitional act. It works only when you will work at it.

Psychologist William James once said, "When you don't feel the way you ought to act, if you just act the way you ought to feel, then you will feel the way you ought to act!"

I once suggested an affirmation to a group of university students: "Every hour on the hour say to yourself, 'I believe in the Power of the Living God.'"

Several put this affirmation into practice. So did I. And during the period in which we voluntarily and scrupulously observed this technique or a close approximation of it, our days took on a new orderliness and design for good.

Try it for a few days—or a few weeks—and see what happens to you and to your life. Is it too simple for your type of mind? Then during the moment of meditation follow whatever philosophical path leads you into a deeper knowledge of Eternal Reality. Make this moment your moment with God, and bring into it the greatest declaration of faith of which you are capable. It is through religious practices that we enter into spiritual consciousness.

What to Do When You Feel All Is Lost

A New York businessman had reached the end of the rope. Life had gotten him down. Mentally, physically, and economically he felt that he was whipped. A will to believe in the world and the life within? He did not have the spiritual faith or the stamina for believing it.

But one day as he stood at his window high over the restless street, as he darkly contemplated the mess he had made of things and the seeming hopelessness of tomorrow, a thought came to him. It was so naive that he put it from his mind. It kept returning. It was a question composed of four simple words, "What would Jesus do?" Finally, under the insistence of the question, he sat down in his swivel chair and said thoughtfully to himself, "What would Jesus do in my case?" As he sat there completely absorbed by the thought, an answer came to him. It might not have been the answer that would have come to you or to me, but it was an answer for him.

He decided to go to the persons involved with him in his little world and talk to them frankly about how he and they could work out their problems. He decided to get a diagnosis of his physical difficulties and calmly do something about it. He was confident that in a mental dilemma of the kind he was in, Jesus would have exercised a will to believe that God is good. He felt sure that Jesus would have considered Himself in a partnership with God, and that is how he, the businessman, determined from then on to play the game.

In his testimony he stated, "I remade my life through this technique. Whenever seemingly insurmountable problems or difficulties presented themselves, I retired to a quiet place and asked myself, 'What would Jesus do?'" The answer, the solution to his difficulties, would always come, sometimes quickly, sometimes after a period of long personal inquiry and self-examination.

Have You Ever Tried the Unusual?

I met a man at a laymen's conference, and across the breakfast table he told me an interesting personal story.

"One day," he recounted, "as I sat in church, dreamily listening to the sermon, I asked myself a question. 'In what way,' I wondered, 'is my life different from that of men who never go to church? What have I ever done that is unusual or startlingly *religious?*' I had listened to hundreds of sermons and had attended countless services, but how had the gospel ever taken hold of my heart?

"I couldn't think of a single, solitary instance," he confessed to me, "in which I truly felt I was different from anyone else. While thinking about this, I noticed in the pew in front of me a small pledge card and a pencil, neatly sharpened, conveniently nearby. I picked up the card and the pencil and musingly I wrote after the dollar sign, "$5,000," just to see what it would look like. Then I signed my name. While I sat there contemplating this, the ushers suddenly moved down the aisles with their collection trays. Absently I dropped the pledge card into the tray.

"That afternoon," he went on, "there was a banging at my door. There stood the minister. 'Tell me,' he said excitedly, holding the pledge card in his hand, 'what's the meaning of this? Did you mean fifty dollars, or maybe five hundred? It says five thousand dollars!' I told him that was correct. What was he so excited about? Wasn't that what he had always been preaching? Hadn't he asked us to 'step out with God?' Okay, that's what I was doing. Stepping out with God. It was one of the great moments of my life."

It was a technique.

38

The Lord's Side of the Ledger

I once told a group of ministers that when I started out in my own parish I preached tithing so hard I almost started to tithe myself! There's a thought here. You cannot give others something you do not have. You cannot persuade others to do something which you have not tested in the laboratory of your own life. It was not until I did tithe that I was able to persuade others that tithing would be a usable technique for modern Christian living.

A man came into a bank to borrow seven thousand dollars, and when the banker was making out the deposit slip the borrower said, "Just a moment. I want seven hundred dollars of the loan put into a separate account."

"Very well," said the banker, "whose account is that?"

"The Lord's," replied the borrower.

Incidentally, when the banker told me this story he confessed, "I thought I had hold of a crackpot for sure. Isn't it rather unusual for a man to tithe on a loan?" But he admitted that through the years the "crackpot" had become one of the town's leading and most respected businessmen.

Does that mean that everyone should tithe on a loan? No. There are degrees of faith, and one man may carry his faith and spiritual experimentation and his will to believe further than another. It is up to you how far you will extend your faith.

39

We Have a Heritage the Moment
We Come into the World

Each of us is given a heritage and a legacy the moment we come into this world: talents, time, life. What we do with these possessions, how we invest them, determines what we are.

The successful people, the great people, in the terms by which we have defined greatness, are not supermen. They are people like you and me who have been willing to work long and hard in the realm of the world and the life within.

They knew that in their life there were no limitations, no lack of supply, no restrictions on how far they might go or what they might be in living up to the highest and greatest and best that they could visualize. They knew that nothing could hold them back except their lack of a will to believe.

Is this spiritual self-promotion? Yes, but it is also and always self-denial. You cannot truly have one without the other. We give without thought of a wish to gain, yet we cannot help but gain when we give. The poor Mexican who got so fabulously rich had a motto. He said, "God gives to Borda and Borda gives to God!"

We give friendship and we gain friends. We help others and we are helped. As we radiate health we become healthier. It is the law of the life within. Will to believe it. Will to believe the role in life you are to play is *your* role. Will to believe that you are equipped to play it because it is the inner you, and it will not be long before that *you* is realized.

4. Steps to Self=Expression!

Do you want to practice a technique? Here is one I learned from a follower of Yoga. Take a walk quietly by yourself. Every time you take a step take a deep inhalation. Do this on your first four steps, which means four deep inhalations without exhaling. Then on your next four steps exhale in rhythm with those four steps. Now include with the first four inhalations these words: "God . . . is . . . with . . .me." With each step and with each inhalation, say one of those words. Do the same during the exhalation. Walk around a block, rhythmically breathing and pronouncing the words and see for yourself what this does in the way of bringing you into a deepening religious consciousness. You will feel free, relaxed, and in tune with the universe.

45

Walking with God

I suggested this technique to a devout Christian friend. He told me later that he got "better results" when he substituted for "God is with me," the words, "I love Je-sus, I love Je-sus," keeping this in the rhythmic pattern of the four breaths. Why should I have dictated *what* he could say? Each person might well figure out an affirmation according to his type of mind, just so long as he walks and breathes and talks with God!

The close relationship between controlled breathing and spiritual consciousness is, of course, as old as religion itself. Hinduism has kept it alive and practiced it and many of the new faiths place strong emphasis upon it. We do not breathe deeply enough. We do not breathe thoughtfully enough. We do not breathe religiously enough, nor do we breathe as if the breath of our life and the breath of God's life were one and the same, as, indeed, they are.

If this one simple and elementary "Yoga hint" should lead you further into a study of the art of breathing, I am sure it will also lead you into a deeper awareness of the world and the life within you.

The True Meaning of Prayer

What is true of the technique of breathing is also true of prayer. We do not know how to pray. If prayer is simply a matter of shutting one's eyes and rattling off

46

a few words before meals or before going to bed, it is an illusion. Prayer, if it is anything at all, is communion with the consciousness of God *within you*. Many people who would be offended if you accused them of believing in an anthropomorphic God still pray to one. There is no religious technique so abused, so abased and so much misunderstood as the technique of prayer.

How often has someone said to you, "Now, you just pray about this," while you had no idea what prayer meant or how prayer operated in your life?

Next time someone says this to you, ask him, "How does a person pray?"

How to Understand What Prayer Is

There are some people who should readily understand the technique of prayer. The musician should understand it because prayer is like committing some immortal composition into mind and heart. This is not done by putting your violin under your chin and half-heartedly fiddling through the number. It is not done by daydreaming or wishing that it weren't all so difficult and complex. You do not learn that number in any other way than by absorbing it into your very soul, until it becomes a part of you and you become a part of it. Only when you have been over-powered by it, can it over-power you.

Prayer is like that. Prayer is a yearning and a striving

47

and a closing out of the world, until whatever you are praying for or about becomes a living reality in the world and the life within.

An artist ought to understand what prayer is, for it is a deeply creative expression. He will say it is something that tugs at your heart and will not let you rest until you have given it form. It haunts you and tortures you and calls you back time and time again to your canvas, and you work with it and fashion it until it becomes a living thing.

A lover ought to understand prayer, for it is, as so often has been said, "the soul's sincere desire, uttered or unexpressed." I have seen this written on the faces of the monks as they stood motionless before the object of their affection, and I have felt it as I knelt nearby while they lay prostrate on the abbey floor, lost in prayer. If prayer is not a mystical experience it is nothing. It is a cry of love that comes from the deepness of the world and life within.

A mother ought to understand prayer, for prayer is compassion. It is nothing if it is not compassion, selfless, solicitous, and unconcealed compassion. It must be that, for what can be more pagan than to pray without compassion? Whether it is a prayer of adoration or supplication or what you will, prayer is surely compassion.

It is in this moment that you embrace not only God, but all of life—life with its many wasted and warped and twisted strands; in that moment of prayer you hold

48

them in your hands and smooth them out. You cannot speak of evil, for in that transfigured and fleeting and breathless time you have touched something—not above and beyond, but *within*.

You are part of the creative process, you are part of the world with all that the world is and means; it is prayer that has joined you with all its sufferings and its joys.

A doctor ought to know what prayer is when he holds life in his hands. A soldier ought to know what it is when, in that awful moment of conflict between his life and another's, all life becomes suddenly holy. A miner ought to know what prayer is when he stands inside the earth and hears nothing and sees nothing except the endless dark, and knows even as he stands there that in that dark is endless light.

The seaman, the traveler, the scientist, the aviator, the farmer, the laborer, the man who has more of this world's goods than he deserves and the man who has less than he deserves; each ought to know what prayer is because of that moment when he suddenly sees himself as he really is, when he enters into the sanctuary of his own soul and speaks to God—and listens as God speaks to him.

Here Is How a Man Prays

When a man prays, he unlocks a door. He enters his

49

own chamber, the chamber of his heart. He closes the door behind.

He says, "I am now going to explore the God-consciousness in me. It may be that I will not even know what to say. It may be that I will have no words at all, only thoughts and impressions, and hopes and fears, and faith and questioning, but this is my moment for communion, and I know that I shall find Him there and that when I abandon my will to His will my prayer will have been said."

Can you think of any other, any more "reasonable reason" for prayer than that it puts your true self in harmony with God? Those who think of prayer or of affirmations as some systematic trick or modern magic to make God a servitor surely miss the point. Prayers and affirmations are means to an end, and the end is a consecrated life. They are "handles of power" and not the power itself.

If you honestly ask, "What will prayer do for me?" there is but one honest answer, "Pray and see."

Shall We Believe in Miracles?

You must will to believe that God exists within you, that it is possible for you to commune with Him, and that there is no limit to what this spiritual adventure may lead to in the way of good. For we must believe in "miracles," and we must believe that he who believes in

50

them does not need them to uphold his will to believe. A miracle is a miracle only to the uninitiated. It is never miraculous to the initiate, and it is always within the framework of immutable law.

Let me give you an example. When I interviewed Therese Neumann, the stigmatist of Konnersreuth, Germany, I was willing to believe that the wounds in her hands were "real." I was equally willing to believe that Therese sustained her physical life and health despite her complete renunciation of food—she actually eats nothing with the exception of the daily sacrament. In short, I was willing to believe, along with a goodly number of professional observers who had kept her under surveillance for long periods at a time, that there was something here which could not be explained by any known law. Therese, buxom and strong when I saw her, had eaten nothing except the small wafer for nearly thirty years.

We call this a miracle, but only because of the inadequacy of language, only because semantically we have no way of saying that a thing is a miracle and is not a miracle at one and the same time. For *if* Therese actually lives "without eating," she has simply gotten hold of a secret or a process within the realm of immutable law, and we gluttons haven't quite caught up with her as yet!

There is a good chance that such a secret and such a process exist. It is fairly well established among Hindu yogis that it is possible to draw nourishment from the

51

air, the sunlight, and contact with the earth. They call this "living by solar energy," and to us who must get our "solar energy" through plant-life and the flesh of animals, it is inconceivable that human life can be sustained in any other way. To us, getting a sufficient quantity of energy in any other way would be miraculous, until we learned how to get it directly from cosmic power. Therese Neumann and certain yogis may already know the secret.

Miracles Defined

It is that way with most "miracles." To the person unfamiliar with electronics, the radio and TV are still miraculous, and to most of us, untutored in the realm of atomic fission, the A- and the H-bomb are the miracles of miracles, for they deal with a force that cannot be seen but which can nonetheless be controlled and harnessed and directed to bless or curse the earth. There is nothing miraculous about it, says the atomic physicist; it is all within the framework of a universal law that can be trusted and depended upon.

"We had many talks about the idea of miracles," says author Ouspensky, "and about the fact that the Absolute cannot manifest its will in our world and that this will manifests itself only in the form of mechanical laws and cannot manifest itself by violating these laws."

To this we can only reply, "Right! But who has ever

52

probed the depth of these laws? Who knows what 'miracles' are hidden there within the law—'miracles' in harmony *with* the laws?"

When someone asks, "Do you believe that Jesus actually performed those so-called miracles?" I must say, "I do. He lived so close to the Source of power, He was such an Adept in the knowledge of God, of the secrets of immutable law and of 'spiritual fission,' about which the average man knows nothing, that our supernatural world was His natural world."

Your Will to Work in the World Within Will Work Its Own "Miracle"

In proportion to the few fleeting moments that most of us spend in this kind of research, we, too, do the work of Jesus. And if we would ever dare, if we should ever have the courage to enter with Him into active and complete harmony with God, then, and only then, would the prophecy be fulfilled that we "shall do even greater things" than He did. We do not yet have the courage. We do not take the time.

We are just now learing the meaning of the will to believe. This is especially true in the ever-growing field of spiritual healing and conversions, prompted by the new research in parapsychology, paraphysics, and soul dynamics generally. Deeply and long hidden "miracles" are being uncovered. One person is able to read a karmic

53

cycle, another finds a source of healing power, and another is able to demonstrate a certain power of "mind over matter." Wherever these manifestations are genuine, you may depend upon it that they operate within an immutable law, God's law.

The "miracle" is so because it is possible for some spiritual explorers to probe into immutable law and discover that it reaches out beyond our vaunted present knowledge.

This is the true magic of faith, and I would not give very much for a religion which did not have this magic and urge its people to try to understand it. It is the magic of a will to believe that there is a life and a world within our own that is God's world and God's life. What we are saying is that spiritual exercises, techniques, and holy habits are methods by which this world and this life may be explored and comprehended.

One Man's Technique

I know a man who has a technique that he calls *anonymity.* He is convinced that the most rewarding act of Christian love and faith is to give without thought of getting, help without wanting help in return, and rewarding others without thought of personal reward —even without the reward of being thanked. Anonymity, he insists, is the physical evidence of spiritual belief, and the true charitable act should always be wholly selfless.

It was only by accident some years ago that I discovered his practice and persuaded him to tell me his story. I caught him red-handed, one dark night, setting a box of groceries on the porch of a needy home. A suspicious character, to say the least, for it was far from Christmas.

"You have no idea what it does to a man," he told me earnestly, "to be Mr. Anonymous."

Had his case been psychoanalyzed and "typed," it would probably have shown some dangerous repressions. But he had his own explanation of his practice.

"I feel," he said, "that a man's religious experience is something so sacred and so personal that he can discuss or demonstrate it only anonymously. I could never be a preacher for that reason. I wouldn't want to air my innermost beliefs. When I hear someone brazenly talking about what religion has done for him, I wonder if it has done anything for him. I'm afraid of evangelists and I'm suspicious of those who carry God on a stick. The good life comes from doing good."

Here Is Your Secret Source of Power

The will to believe in a world and a life within also recognizes that there is a power generated in contemplation. This does not necessarily mean retiring to a

55

cloister or withdrawing from the world. It means, rather, harmonizing your thoughts about yourself and your life with the thought of God.

Contemplation is the condition of love in one's heart. Everyone in love knows how the object of his love possesses him and how there is scarcely a moment when the image of the loved one is not present. There are those who love money so much that their entire contemplation is centered upon it. They think, eat, dream, and sleep —money.

Others do the same with art, travel, or achievement of one sort or another; with family, friends, bridge, beauty, health, prominence, sex—just about anything can become the object of one's affection. And there are those who love God that much. Their contemplation is on Him and on His will for their lives.

"Whoever has God in mind," Eckhart once said, "simply and solely God, in all things, such a man carries God with him into all his works and into all places, and God alone does all his works. He seeks nothing but God, nothing seems good to him but God. He becomes one with God in every moment."

This comradeship is at the heart of contemplation, and we ought by rights to develop it more. It asks nothing for itself, it wants no self-promotion and no material gain, and it makes no religious pretensions. The world desperately needs it, and the only way it can ever be realized is through the individual heart and life.

Facing up to Life's Greatest Challenge

Does this mean that everything in life is then suddenly explained and clarified? Does it mean that we shall no longer have any worry or care? Some people who tithe affirm that ever since they began cheerfully giving a tenth of their income "to the Lord" they have prospered. But I know people who prosper and who never unbegrudgingly give the Lord a dime.

When a mother prays that her soldier son be spared, and he is spared, who can help but wonder about the boy who fell at his side, the boy whose mother was praying just as earnestly for him?

I know a man who was jailed for fifteen years and who for fifteen years maintained his innocence. During those fifteen years of imprisonment, the guilty man was free until a "chance" incident pinned the guilt on him.

Is there a positive way of proving that in the kind of world in which we live everyone gets his just rewards? And have you ever walked the Via Dolorosa without asking yourself why this good Man had to die and what He must have thought as He felt the weight of the cross and the sting of the whips? Why was God's "plan of salvation" so unyielding and so harsh that it nailed this same Man to the cross?

There is only one way in which we can affirmatively accept the universe and all that it holds in the way of these mysteries: a will to believe in the world and the

57

life within. Then we do not try to explain every happening and every event. Then we are no longer upset by every changing circumstance or life's seeming injustices. Then we do not care to say, "Now I know beyond the shadow of a doubt." We do not try to prove or test God. We believe.

Religion then becomes a personal encounter with God, an individual, psychological experience. As Jesus said to Peter, when the latter turned to see what was happening to John, "If I will that he tarry until I come, what is that to thee? Follow thou Me."

Contemplation will remind you: "Religion is my personal meeting with God, the revelation of God for me." You will no longer have any right to judge another's faith or his standard of spiritual values or his interpretation of what is right or wrong for him. Your life is *your* life. Your will to believe that God is good and just and righteous, and your faith that the law of causality is a divine, immutable law, become the gateway through which you enter a well-adjusted, well-poised and well-integrated life for *you*.

How to Deal with Evil

Someone is always saying, "It would be so wonderful if all the people in the churches were good people and all the people outside of the churches were not good. But, as it is, there are so many good people outside the churches and so many bad people in the churches that it all becomes very confusing!"

And, we might add, very wonderful! Here we might ask, what is the basis for a judgment of what is good and what is bad? It is a typically American and, frequently, a typically "Christian" trait to pigeon-hole a person or a condition as either black or white, either all bad or all good.

The truth is that every life is a spectrum, in every life God shines through—and evil shines through, too. The right relationship between the two is established not when evil has ceased to exist, but when goodness exists in such abundance and with such understanding that the evil is lost in the brightness of the good.

In Jagernath, India, where it is customary for loved ones to burn their dead, there is a tomb which is called Kabir's, inscribed upon which is this saying: "O friend, live so with good and bad that, after thy death, the Musselman may wish to bury you and the Hindu to burn thee according to his rite."

The Measure of True Spirituality

The church is the means and not the end of the spiritual quest. There was a day when denominationalism was nonexistent and when even the terms Catholic and Protestant were unknown. Yet in those days, God was walking among men. There is no assurance that the

59

term Catholic and Protestant or any other religious designation will always be with us, but even if they should become totally extinct, God still will be walking among men. "There is only one religion," as Shaw once said, "though there are a hundred versions of it."

It is rather well established that in our colleges and universities today, and among young people generally, there is a lessening concern as to where a man stands in the divergent patterns of the Christian faith, and a noticeable increase as to what the individual is and believes, and by what art he has found the will to believe in the world and the life within.

The relationship between God and man is not vertical, as the common image has it, but circular. There is no separating your life into an arc and God's life into an arc, or contending that, "Here am I . . . and there is God." The life of man and the life of God in man is one life. Kahlil Gibran stated it well when he said,

> Who can separate his faith from his action,
> Or his belief from his occupation?
> Who can spread out his hours before him and say,
> 'This is for God, but this is for myself,
> This is for my soul, but this is for my body?'
> All your hours are wings which beat through space
>   from self to self;
> And he who wears his morality only as his best
>   garment
> Were better naked; the sun and the wind
> Can tear no holes in his skin.
> And he to whom worshipping is a window

60

To open but also to shut,
Has never visited the house of his soul
Whose windows are open from dawn to dawn;
Your daily life is your temple and your religion.*

Live YOUR Life

The will to believe in the world and the life within makes faith personal and vital to each individual. It urges him never to envy, never to judge, never to covet and never to condemn. His world is his. Your world is yours. His life is strictly between himself and God. Your life is strictly between yourself and God.

I know a man who is blind and poor, but I never come away from visiting him without feeling enriched.

I know a man who is physically as perfect as a man can be and very wealthy. I never come away from visiting him without feeling equally enriched.

Each man lives with God humbly according to his station. It is this that judges them. Each is aware of his inner self, his God-self, and each has the will to believe that what he is and what he has are purposeful for him. Each has made the supreme discovery: what we do with the life *within,* in terms of self-realization, self-awareness, self-denial, and self-expression, is our greatest mission during our sojourn here on earth.

---

* Reprinted from *The Prophet,* by Kahlil Gibran, with permission of the publisher, Alfred A. Knopf, Inc. Copyright 1923 by Kahlil Gibran; renewal copyright 1951 by Administrators C. T. A. of Kahlil Gibran Estate, and Mary G. Gibran.

61

Religion's Chief Function

Religion's chief function is not to make a man good or to make a man virtuous or even to make a man a perfect social being. These are religion's by-products. The chief function of religion is to inspire a man to embark on the spiritual adventure and to recognize the "Christ within" as his way of salvation.

Apply yourself to spiritual exercises, religious techniques and the will to believe! Through such media as affirmations, the art of prayer, the challenge of stewardship and contemplation, you close the gap between the unreal superficial you and the YOU that is your real self, the YOU that is God's manifestation in you.

Those who say that it is *not* possible to see God are right inasmuch as He cannot be seen with physical eyes; but those who say it *is* possible to see God are also right, because the rational soul sees him with spiritual vision through a will to believe.

We return to where we began. You are a distinctive, individual expression of a Creative Force. That which makes you YOU is personal, unique, and exclusive. Be yourself according to the world and the life within. You are endowed with a greatness and a talent distinctly God's expression for YOU. The greatest challenge of your life is to make the most of the YOU that is your real self.

Part II

THE WILL TO BELIEVE
IN THE WORLD
AND
THE LIFE AROUND

5. The Will To Believe That Things Always Get Better

W HILE RIDING IN THE SUBWAY THE other day I overheard this conversation:

"How are things with you?"

"Terrible."

"Yes, and they'll get worse."

"Why?"

"They always do."

Now I wish I had had the nerve or the know-how to have said to these two fellows, "How about trying a changed mental attitude for, let's say, thirty days? How about changing your will to believe that the world is *against* you to the will to believe that the world is *for* you? What about starting every day with a will to believe that things always get *better*?"

I probably would have been told, "Put yourself in my place. I've been getting one bad break after another.

I'm realistic. I *know* what's happening to me. Things may not always get worse with you but they always get worse with me."

The Life You Think Is the Life You Live

I'd have agreed. I would even have agreed that the speaker was being realistic. But he is realistic on the side of defeat. He *could* be realistic on the side of success. Would this be easy? No. It would mean work. It would mean the development of a will to believe in the world and the life around. It would mean the will to believe that the relish of life is its uncertainty, its hazards, and its mystery, and a conviction that in and through every circumstance and experience, life is always good to *you.*

A cartoon which my dad had tacked up in his office created one of my earliest impressions. It was the picture of a stork standing on one leg. Beside this wise old bird stood two men. One was tabbed Mr. Pessimist. Looking at the stork, he was saying dubiously, "He's standing on his last leg." The other fellow, Mr. Optimist, was saying, "He's putting his best foot forward."

It was all a matter of a point of view. As far as I have observed through the years, the stork has been doing all right.

One evening, in the Middle East, a group made up of various nationalities was sitting around taking Ameri-

68

cans apart bit by bit. Americans, one said, are too aggressive. Americans, said another, are too opinionated. Americans, a third contended, are isolationists. Americans, a fourth said, are internationalists.

A Syrian, sitting next to me, spoke up, "America is so big and so diversified," he said, "that just about anything you say about it is true."

Anything You Care to Say About the World Is TRUE

That is the way it is with the world. Just about anything you care to say about it is true. You can say that life is good to you or life is bad, that friends are kind or friends are untrue, that you get the good breaks or the bad, that there is more of joy than of sorrow, or more of sorrow than of joy.

You can roam inside the great blue bowl of life and believe just about what you wish to believe, but one thing is sure: what you will to believe about the world and the life *around* becomes the world in which you live. You are, to this degree at least, the creator of the kind of world in which you find yourself, and in it you are the master of your destiny. You are a co-worker with God in this work of creation.

The Will to Believe That the World Around You Is GOOD

If you have the will to believe that the world *within* is good, then, of course, it is just a step for you to believe

69

that the world *around* is also good. For if you will to believe that the life within you is an expression of God's life, then God's life is expressed in everyone, and the joy and sorrow, the triumph and tragedy, the good breaks and bad which you experience are the common experience of everyone.

I doubt very much whether it can be *proved* that the world and the life around you are good. Haven't you often been disappointed—most of all in someone you trusted or wanted to trust? Haven't you ever caught yourself saying, "The more you do for people, the more they expect?" Or, "The best way to lose a friend is to take him into your confidence?" Other people have the same idea. In fact, the proverbs of nations are full of the same impressions:

> "Trust, but not too much." *(German)*
> "Do not trust or contend nor borrow or lend, and you'll gain in the end." *(Spanish)*
> "Swim and don't trust." *(French)*
> "Trust no one until you've eaten a bushel of salt with him." *(Arabic)*
> "Never trust a black Brahmin nor a white Pariah." *(Hindu)*
> "Distrust is the mother of safety." *(Russian)*

One day in a hotel lobby in Mexico City a tourist sat in absolute dejection, dangling a leather purse in his hands. "Look at this," he said to me. "Isn't this enough to make a man lose faith in his fellowman? I just

70

paid three hundred *pesos* for this and it's not even real alligator!"

He went on to tell me that for several days he had a guide whom he liked very much. He liked him so much, in fact, that he began giving him generous tips along the way. The more tips he gave, however, the more the guide expected. And gradually the American tourist began to realize that most of the affection the guide had for him was aimed at his hip pocket.

The climax came with the purchase of the leather purse. The tourist had just bought it at the insistence of the guide and was standing outside the door of the shop when he heard the guide say to the shop owner in Spanish, *"Te dije que era creido."* The tourist remembered the phrase and, back at his hotel, asked the desk clerk for the translation. He got it: "I told you he'd be easy." It was then he discovered that the purse wasn't real alligator!

Why didn't he report the guide or confront him with the facts? He did not have the heart. He wasn't "built that way," he said. He was content to sit in the hotel lobby and brood over the fact that the moment you begin to trust someone and like someone and help someone, you are in for disillusionment.

You can take such an attitude toward life and your life will be a reflection of your cynicism. Or you can will to believe that the great world around is still good and cooperative and trustful. Then your life will be a

71

reflection of your confidence. And the proverbs of nations are full of this attitude as well.

"Good always finds good, and trust begets trust."
(English)
"He who has never trusted, has never been near to God." *(Serbian)*
"See nothing without seeing God therein." *(Persian)*
"Trust opens many a stubborn door." *(Hindu)*
"A little faith sets most things right." *(French)*

The Most Common of All Life Situations: Confidence Betrayed

Someone once figured out that there are only twelve original plots in playwriting. Every play that has ever been written is based upon one of twelve situations, and the one most often used is that of "confidence betrayed." The eternal triangle wherein one party finds the other to be unfaithful; the eternal other angles in which the town populace awakes one morning to learn that the trusted banker has absconded with their savings; the nation sold out by its leader, the tourist taken in by his friendly guide, the father disappointed in his son—these are all part of the same theme: confidence betrayed.

The greatest drama ever enacted was based on this plot. It reached its climax one night when thirteen men were seated around a table. They had been partners for a long time, comrades in all sorts of experiences, pioneers

in introducing to the world a new idea in the relationship of man to man, and man to God.

Suddenly the leader of the group, looking around the
table at those whom he trusted and loved, said, "One
of you will betray me."

That was the plot: confidence betrayed. The denoue-
ment came quickly after that; the kiss in the garden,
the trial, the crucifixion. And at that point darkness
hung over the earth, as it always does when the will to
believe in a world and a life around goes wrong. Darkness. At that point we always say, "Let's be realistic.
Let's take the world as it really is. Someone is bound to
betray you if you trust him too far. It's human nature.
Be on the alert. Don't take anyone at his word. Look
for some deeply hidden meaning in everyone's action.
If Jesus had only been smart, there'd have been no Golgotha." Darkness.

When We Are Betrayed, What Shall We Do?

But in this greatest drama ever played, the curtain
does not go down forever on Golgotha. It comes up on
a garden. And in that garden is an open tomb. Light
is in that tomb and an angel is standing there. The angel
has a beautiful line to speak in this Play of Plays. It
says, "Why seek ye the living among the dead?"

Something like that happens to a man when he has a
will to believe in the world and the life around. There

73

is a light that shines through the darkness of his disillusionment, and amid all the frustration and despair and hurt, something says to him, "He is not here. This Man, this One with the great ideal who trusted others so very much, this One who brought us a new concept of what life in all its greatest value is like—you do not find Him among the dead and dying beliefs of the past. He is not here. He has risen."

And you catch yourself feeling that it does not matter too much whether anyone put anything over on you, or whether this one got the better of you, or whether perhaps you trusted him more than good judgment allowed. There is a life and a world around that becomes dazzlingly bright, and only those who have the will to believe in it can ever know this world and this life and understand it.

Your Life Is Interwoven with Other Lives

He knew what it was, this Man who bore the cross. He knew what believing in the world and the life around meant in all its pain and glory. And when you learn to enter that world, that "world around" in which you with all your thoughts and passions and desires are the main protagonist, then you will know it, too.

You will then say to yourself, "I have a life to live that is *my* life. But it is interwoven with the lives of others. No man can live unto himself; he has always

74

been and he must always be part of all that he meets and all that he experiences. What I need is a will to believe that those whom I meet and the things that I experience are *good.*"

Is there material reward in this? Not always. Is there really glory in it? It doesn't always seem so. Is it realistic? Not according to our standards. It is an ideal and it has its meaning in the spirit of man. It is the life *within* projected into the life *around,* finding its own and making other lives its own, and bringing into a common collective force the now dispersed and dissipated kindred spirits who also will to believe that the world and the life around us can be good to all.

Is it easy to affirm this will to believe? No, it is difficult. We have erred in thinking that it requires no effort. We have erred even more because we have felt that every condition and every demand of life would have to be realized before we could exercise this will. We must see that it is an act of faith.

We simply *will to believe* that the world around us is good and begin to live as if our belief were true. And if we are betrayed, what then? Then we take up our cross and we go, if need be, as He went, into the darkness, and through the darkness into the light.

6. The Will to Believe
In a United World

ON CHRISTMAS EVE, TWO YEARS AGO, I attended a church service in the Russian sector of Berlin. The hotel clerk in West Berlin cautioned me about the trip but added, "At Christmas time you will not have the difficulty you might have at other times. The spirit of Christmas gets over the Russian line."

How to Adjust to the World Around

He was right. I encountered no special inconvenience. But the walk from the East Berlin station, where I got off, to *Marien Kirche* was a long and lonely trek. The streets, haunted by rubble and plastered with signs that read, "With hammer and sickle, with book and gun, forward into socialism," were dead calm. The air was as heavy as the leaden sky. No sound of carols, no laughter, no Christmas trees, no lighted candles, no hurrying shopper nor any other well-known symbol of the season was in evidence. I felt I was walking in the house of the dead.

Marien Kirche was crowded to the doors, and the Red watchers stood stern and aloof as if to say, "Well, if you must have this day, have it and get it over with."

I went in. The church was cold. The people sat huddled in the pews and on the backless benches, too despondent, it seemed to me, to expect a miracle even at this holy time. Silent and resigned they sat waiting for the service to begin. They were poorly dressed and cold; their faces were lined with pain. Near the bare wall, where I found a place, an elderly woman clasped a young boy jealously in her arms as if he were her sole possession.

I looked in vain for young people among these five or six hundred Christian faithful, and I tried without success to find one person who reflected the joy that makes this holy day the happiest of our liturgical year.

Most eyes were fastened upon a *creche*, simply fashioned and set near the chancel area, and the question which these captive worshipers were asking was the one which I was asking, too, "Is it really possible for religion to solve a global problem? Or is religion, at best, only a personal experience, of which we are expecting too much when we ask it to unite a divided world? Should we even hope that it can break our chains, or should we be content that it helps us to endure our chains without complaint, so that we may live passively in relation to every circumstance?"

As I sat there I remembered what many Germans had told me. They said they realized that their nation was suffering because of its sins. Retribution had come upon them with a vengeance.

And yet in the eternal cycle of history all nations have their sins, and it was difficult for me, there in *Marien Kirche*, to think in terms of anything except the separateness of the individual. Each of these worshipers, not as a citizen of a nation, but as an entity in himself, as a separate human being, possessed all the feeling and hope and passion which were also mine as I vicariously shared his present lot. Had these people developed an insensibility to pain which I, fresh from the land of freedom, could not fully grasp? Were they immune to suffering? Or had they perhaps found something in suffering which mitigated it and gave them a source of inner strength? No. They were individuals who felt with all the intensity of any freedom-loving creature the same frenzied resistance to anything which sought to keep them enslaved.

Can the Will to Believe Work the Miracle?

I thought of something else, something that everyone frequently thinks about and hesitates to express because

81

it is too naive, too simple, too impractical, and, if you will, too "stupid" for words. But nonetheless, we often think about it, and I did in *Marien Kirche*. I said to myself, "What would happen if the leaders of all countries concerned could sit here with me at this Christmas service and see what I am seeing and feel what I am feeling? And what would happen if they would suddenly join hands and each would say, 'I will to believe that we can reconcile our differences and live in freedom and in peace! I will to believe that we can break the chains and release the captives and tear down the curtains of hate!'"

Even as I thought of this, I reprimanded myself by saying, "How unrealistic can you be? Do you think that thoughts can work the miracle?"

Then the minister, Propst D. Gruber, came in. Songs were sung, songs of the Christmastide which are never without hope and never without the hint of childlike faith. One must hear *Silent Night* in such a setting, in the land where it was written, to understand how idealistic and full of the divine nature of things it really is.

> Silent night! holy night!
> Darkness flies, all is light;
> Shepherds hear the angels sing:
> 'Alleluia! hail the King!
> Christ the Saviour is born,
> Christ the Saviour is born.'

It is at such a moment that one feels almost justified

in believing that there is no problem, however great, which cannot be solved by a simple will to believe in the world and the life around. Haven't you ever felt this way? Haven't you ever reached out and touched something so startlingly beautiful and so simple that you feel it could solve all problems, however complex, if only enough people had the will to believe?

Our Deepest Thoughts Are Often the Echo of a Universal Longing

Such thoughts suggest themselves to us at the strangest times and in the strangest places, too. At night, sometimes, when in the quiet of the moonlight, we wish that the peace in our hearts could become the peace in all the world. Or when we sit with our families around the table, a table so rich and bounteous that we instinctively say, "Let's have a word of prayer," and our prayer is that everyone might have the thrill and joy of being at such a table with those he loves.

Sometimes these thoughts and the will to believe need nothing more than a beautiful scene, or the open road, or sudden laughter, as if freedom could be had simply for the asking. Sometimes this thought comes to us when we are struck by the terror and absurdity of men killing men for a foot of earth or a coast line.

We often think of this. We all do. We often ask

83

ourselves what would happen if leaders who held the power of nations in their hands would be brave enough, each in his own way and in his own land, to say to the others, "Let us have a will to believe in the world and the life around." I thought of it in *Marien Kirche* in East Berlin and I wondered why we could not make the race for peace as stimulating and intense as we now have made the race for arms.

And I thought of it when I walked through the Mandelbaum Gate, that strip of No Man's Land between Jordan and Israel, and found both Arab and Jew so wonderfully kind to me. How I wished for the magic word which would unite these divided people in the heart of the Holy Land!

Now who would dare say that an attitude, a volitional one at that, an assumed one, let us say, could solve the seemingly irresolvable difficulty between Jew and Arab? Yet, I could not help wondering what would happen if both Arab and Jewish patrol would decide to walk 150 feet, each extend a hand to the other, and say, "I have the will to believe in you. What I want for myself is what you want, freedom and peace and a chance to live fully and richly in this holy land." Nothing more than that to begin with—no diplomatic overtures, no protocols, no legislative manifestos—nothing more for the moment than the outstretched hand and the will to believe in the world and the life around.

84

The Idea That War Can End War Is Obsolescent

I do not know how or when the barbed wire barricade, which is the Mandelbaum Gate, will become an avenue of unity and peace, but somewhere in the solution there will need to be a will to believe in the other fellow.

I do not know how the iron curtain or the bamboo curtain or the dollar curtain can be raised so that there will be trust and faith instead of suspicion and fear, but whenever this is achieved, a will to believe in the world and the life around will have to appear somewhere in the process. This is the new hope, for the idea that war can ever end war is obsolescent, and this is also true of the idea that fear can ever drive out fear.

Let us agree that a global glance at the world is enough to convince anyone that universal goodness is illusory. Nations do not have the will to believe in other nations, individuals do not have the will to believe in other individuals.

But let us also agree that as each of us stands on his side of his curtain, he says, "If only the other person had the will to believe in me! If only he would see things my way!"

We Cannot Prove That There Is Universal Goodness

No, we cannot prove that. We can only prove that there is a widespread conviction that it is the *other* person who is wrong! It is that difficult to detach ourselves

85

from ourselves and to look at ourselves objectively. If we could, we would say, "I am part of whatever goodness and whatever badness exists."

I am sure that anyone who has traveled has heard a tourist say, "I don't like to go to this place or that place. There are too many tourists there." No tourist wants to think that he is just another tourist. He wants to feel that he is different from the rest.

"There's nothing wrong with the world," another says, "nothing wrong at all, except the people in it." When he says that he stands apart, above the passing parade, and cannot see himself as one of the people who might be helping to make the very kind of a world he is criticizing. "Most Americans," we say, "are this or that. Most Americans do this or that." And we say it almost as if we ourselves were a special American type, above and apart from all that makes America what it is.

"The first thing the intellect does with an object," says psychologist William James, "is to class it along with something else. But any object that is infinitely important to us and awakens our devotion feels to us also as if it must be *sui generis* and unique. Probably a crab would be filled with a sense of personal outrage if it could hear us class it without ado or apology as a crustacean, and thus dispose of it. 'I am no such thing,' it would say, 'I am MYSELF, MYSELF ALONE.' " *

---

* From *Varieties of Religious Experience*, by William James. Reprinted by permission of Paul R. Reynolds & Son.

86

My Dog Mike Taught Me a Great Lesson

Mike is a wire-haired terrier, nine years old. Through-out his charmed and thrill-packed life, he has never learned that he is a dog. Dog applies to every other dog but not to him. At mention of the word be becomes furious, rushes to this window and that, barks and shows displeasure at the very thought that some despicable creature—a dog—might venture on his premises. Some-thing in my upbringing of Mike was faulty, of that I'm sure. He doesn't know he's a dog. He's Mike. He sleeps on a chair or on a bed. He has the run of the house. He has a vocabulary of thirty words. And I am sure I read his mind correctly when I say that to Mike there is nothing wrong with the world, nothing at all, except the dogs that are in it. If they could only all be as he is —or as he thinks he is—what a wonderful world it would be.

But the more I study Mike from my high station of *homo sapiens,* the more I realize that it would be a sad day for the world of dogs if they were all as impudent and as opinionated and as independent as Mike. And I have often wondered whether God, looking at us from a station infinitely higher in proportion than mine is to Mike, may have the same feeling about us humans. Sometimes this makes me quite humble! Indeed, when I let the thought sink in, I realize that the best thing I can do is to admit that I am what I am where I am, and

87

it is time I develop a will to believe that the world and the life around are made up of many ME's. I am one with them and they are one with me. When I think of life in this relationship I become a new being and I cease to judge whether the other fellow is better or worse than I. In fact, I then reach the conclusion that people are not on a higher or lower level than I. They are only different. And I am different, too. And I would much rather take the chance that my will to believe in the other person should lead me to occasional disillusionment than to dedicate myself to a will to disbelieve in him and be led to cynicism about the world and the life around.

7. How to Develop Your Personal Will to Believe

WOULD YOU LIKE TO TRY AN EXPERI-
ment in the will to believe in the world and the life
around?

Is someone making life unpleasant for you or giving
you a hard time?

Then here's the experiment. Go into your room or into
a quiet place and shut yourself off from all outside dis-
traction. Sitting alone, or standing or kneeling alone,
close your eyes and bring into mental image the person
who is making your days confused.

As you visualize this person and hold the image in
mind, also bring into focus whatever your idea of God
may be. I doubt that you can visualize God in any
tangible form since God is a Spirit. He is *the* Spirit of
everything that is creative and good. He is Primal Cause

and Cosmic Consciousness. He is Love and Sensitivity and Understanding. He is the ultimate realization of the "imperfect perfection" within each of us. Visualize Him as best you can. I sometimes think it would be impossible for me to develop any mental image of God were it not for Jesus. The virtues and the personality of the Galilean are those I associate intimately with God. Indeed, you may be one of those who believe that Jesus was actually God walking among men.

A Technique for Treating Your Enemies

Now in your moment of experimentation look at your "enemy," as it were, through the image of God and say to yourself words somewhat like these, "This person is made in the likeness of God just as I am. He is subject to the same laws of life, he is the receiver of the same blessings and the victim of the same circumstances that are mine, that are everyone's; the same mortality, the same hope for immortality, the same entrance into this world and the same exit from this world are ours. He is not perfect, but neither am I perfect. He is not entirely in the wrong, neither am I. But even if he were, for this brief moment I see him through the image of God."

Let the impression of these thoughts sink in and possess you. Then during these moments will to think good thoughts about him. Will to believe that the relationship between you can and will improve, that you can understand each other, and that you can learn to respect each other. In these moments, send thoughts of charity and understanding out to him. For a little while see him in a new light, see him in the image of God, even as you see yourself, too, in God's image.

Now what do you think will happen? How do you suppose you will feel after some five or more minutes of sincere meditation in this realm of good? Deep inside of you there will be a sense of cleansing. Deep in your heart will be a feeling of peace. The mind is calmed and a new and vivid instinct arises: a conviction that this is not merely some kind of mental hokus-pokus or departure into white magic, but that a mystical power has been generated which actually becomes a source of influence in the experimental realm of human relations.

As one man put it, "The next time I met the person *with* whom I had been praying, a change had taken place between us."

He was right. In the quiet of his room he was actually praying *with* his "enemy." He was going further than merely praying *for* those who despitefully used him. He was bringing his antagonist along with himself into God's fellowship.

The World Around You IS a Thought-World

Most of us do not work sufficiently in the realm of the unseen. Most of us neglect almost entirely the world of

93

the subconscious in its relation with the world and the life around us. The unseen world is the world of thought, desire, and intention, of conscience and spirit put into harmony with the conscience and spirit of others through the will to believe. It is, to reiterate, the world within reaching out into the world around.

I was in two homes recently, one old and one new, one Protestant and one Catholic, and each had a special "chapel room." The Protestant owner referred to his room as his "prayer corner;" the Catholic spoke of his as his "oratorio." Each had its characteristic Christian symbols. Each had a small altar and in the oratorio burned a votive light. The stories the owners told me were identical.

"We wanted a quiet place," they said, "to which we could retire for meditation."

"A good psychological device," a friend of mine commented when I told him about these places and mentioned that the idea was fast taking hold in other homes. "A good psychological device," he quipped. "Every home ought to have one. Hamlet said to Ophelia, 'Get thee to a nunnery.' We could say to friend wife, 'Get thee to the prayer corner.' I know lots of families that could stand a foxhole like that!"

In return I had to contend that it was not only a good psychological device, but a good mystical device, too, for we are not talking about a fictionalized world when we talk about a will to believe. We are not reducing the intellect to credulity. We are talking about a potential world in which we may realize ideal values and achieve the highest possible good. And who will deny that a will to believe has been in the vanguard of every great march toward a better life?

Depend upon it: the world around you is a thought-world. There is a power generated in prayer, and an actual empathic force that rises out of the restoration of a will to believe in the world and the life around. Many a marital rift could be healed if the people concerned, even one of them, sincerely practiced a will to believe in the other person. There is no one who can hold back the mystical power generated through honest compassion and genuine love.

William Law once said, "There is nothing makes us love a man as much as praying for him."

Thoughts and Ideas Have Power and Force

One evening I visited with a group of young Americans in the bombed-out city of Kassel, Germany. These were members of the Church of the Brethren, a pacifistic denomination which has done a remarkably unselfish and unacclaimed work of rehabilitation, particularly in Germany and in Greece. The young men and women were donating a few years of their life in an attempt to rebuild lives and re-establish faith in highly neglected and needy areas. Pacifists they were at heart, but the

95

grim problem of how to deal with "gangster leaders and gangster nations" was a thorny one. How realistic is this theory of meeting violence with an ideal? How do you stop an actual physical attack with faith and prayer?

As we were discussing these things, one of the young men spoke up. "What we need," he said, "is a belief in a mystical power. Either there is a power which can be tapped and which stands with us when we live according to our Christian ideals, or there isn't. Either we generate a power for good or we don't. We can distribute all the food and clothing in the world, but unless we have a will to believe that the spirit of the other fellow can be influenced by our spirit and our faith, we are missing the point."

To him there was a disturbing anomaly in Christendom: although we admit that legalized murder—war—is incompatible with the code of Christ, we do not have the will to believe that there can be any other avenue to peace. What he was saying is that our attitudes embody not only "good psychology" but a mystical power, a power which cannot be measured because it has never been tried or put to its ultimate test on a global scale. That is what thinking people everywhere are saying. And they are asking when we will be courageous enough to believe that what happens between us and the person we took with us into our "prayer corner" can also happen between nations. *Nations are but groups of individuals.*

96

MacArthur came very near to the sum and substance of this when, in his Los Angeles address, he said, "Must we fight again before we learn? When will some great figure in power have sufficient imagination and moral courage to translate this universal wish, which is rapidly becoming universal necessity, into actuality? We are in a new era! The old methods and solutions no longer suffice. We must have new thoughts, new ideas, new concepts. We must break out of the strait jacket of the past. There must always be one to lead, and we should be that one. We should now proclaim our readiness to abolish war in concert with the great powers of the world. The result might be magical."

Perhaps, as we stated in our opening paragraphs, since the world has gone forward with its "heretics" and its "non-conformists," it will also rise with its "idealists" and with its "visionaries."

Life Is That Great and Noble Game

Life, to the average man, is a game. A great and noble game. An adventure. He believes in rules and codes, and he admires sportsmanship. To try to make life more orderly, more equitable, and more productive are some of his natural aims. Anything that can help bring about these results, whether it is a management-labor conference in which he has a stake or an international conference at Geneva in which he has an interest, is a step

97

in the climb toward realizable ideals. At every level of experience, in every phase of living, the courage of the quest prompts him to say, "Keep alive the will to believe in the world and the life around!"

A man from Sweden, who was visiting me recently, said, "My country lies in fully as precarious a geographical position as does Germany. But we have had a hundred and forty years of peace simply and solely for one reason. Our people have a will to believe that peace is possible."

How do we get that way? By beginning in our own little "prayer corner," by spending time in our own private "oratorio," and by conquering our personal "enemies" through the mystical, usable power that we generate *as we become aware that it exists.*

I have seen this power at work on every level of society. I have seen relationships improve between individuals and groups in homes, in colleges, in industry, and wherever life's problems were tackled with an earnest and unshaken will to believe. And because I have seen this empirical and "miraculous" evidence in others, I know that it will also work in you and me. Give it attention, experimentation, and time and you will find an ever-expanding and ever more effective meaning in the world and the life around you.

8. Ring Up the Curtain on a New World

I ASKED AN ENDURANCE SWIMMER, "HOW is it possible for you to swim for twenty hours? What kind of mental attitude do you have?"

She said, "I believe that the water is a friend. It wants to help me. It does not fight against me and I do not fight against it. We are working together."

How NOT to Fight Life

I often think of that when I am in the "swim" of life. The waves and the currents and the tides hit us all at times, and it is not always easy to say, "The water is friendly." It requires an act of faith, a volitional act; it means work, but most of all it requires a will to believe. The more we use this will, the more it becomes a part of us and the more natural becomes its application.

101

An octogenarian, who has shipped around the world a good deal, who has adventured in primitive areas more than anyone I know, gave me this sound advice, "Don't ever get panicky in the woods, on the water, or in the air. Nature and you are both God's expression. You were made for each other. No matter where you are, always feel at home."

You can ring up the curtain on a new world by a simple act of faith. Will to believe that the world and the life around you are assisting, not opposing you. How do you do this? Must you wait until you can find proof that this is true? No. You simply say to yourself, "I will to believe! From now on I begin to live as if this were true." And it is true as long as you believe it. It is untrue, for you, when you begin to disbelieve it.

The director of a college theatre in a midwestern town told me an amazing story.

"I was vacationing in Arizona," he said, "and one day my seven-year-old son came to me and pulled a snake out of his pocket. 'What kind of snake is this, daddy?' he asked. I didn't know. 'Some harmless snake, I suppose,' I told him, 'or you wouldn't be carrying it around that way. What do you want to do with it?' 'Take it home,' said the boy. I agreed. Like many another kid, he was all the time playing the naturalist with frogs and beetles and what-not. So we brought the snake back home to Iowa with us. One day I decided to get the lowdown on

102

this pet, so I took it to a biology professor at the college. Putting the snake on his desk, I said, 'What kind of a reptile is this?' He instinctively raised his voice in astonishment. 'Why man!' he exclaimed, 'that's a deadly Arizona coral!' When he said that, I drew back and the snake struck at me."

What law, what instinct kept it from striking previously? What impulse, what "adrenalin betrayal" did my friend unwittingly release in that unguarded moment? Why do rattlesnakes strike at white men but never touch an Indian? How does my dog, Mike, instinctively know whom he can trust and of whom he must be suspicious? How am I to explain that I met a voodooist in Haiti who as a rule resented outsiders, yet said cordially, "I was expecting you!"

The World Sends Back Your Thoughts in Kind

There is a world and a life around us which sends back our thoughts in kind. The coin of its realm is the coin we give it. Its faith in us is a reflection of our faith in it. Will to believe that this world is good and cooperative and you will find it to be so. Ring up this curtain on your new world!

Suspicion breeds suspicion, faith gives rise to faith. Fear spawns fear, confidence generates confidence. Life is too short, too adventurous, too packed with beauty and

103

joy, for us to spend one hour in negative darkness with the curtain down. Remember—the basis of all life is the will to believe.

Unrealistic? Hardly! In the best-selling, most-loved, and most-read Book in the world are the words: "Except ye become like little children, ye shall in no wise enter the Kingdom of Heaven."

Do you remember how bright and thrilling the world used to be in those days when we were children and when we walked and lived by faith? What has happened to us? Did we have to forfeit this will to believe as our penalty for growing up? Not at all. What we need is simply a new determination to hold on to our ideals and never to let go of our dreams.

"Out in the alley, up in an attic, or down in the barn or lying along the waterside, a child always dreams, and the dreams are real. So Thomas Edison dreamed. So Robert Louis Stevenson dreamed. So Sir Walter Scott dreamed. And out of the stuff of such magic dreams are woven some of the finest and most beautiful fabrics we have ever seen." So said philosopher Lin Yutang.*

And of ideals and the fight to hold on to them, the renowned Albert Schweitzer declared, "As one who tries to remain youthful in his thinking and feeling, I have struggled against facts and experience on behalf of belief in the good and the true. At the present time when violence dominates the world, I still remain convinced

---

* From *The Importance of Living* (New York: John Day Co., Inc., 1937).

that truth, love, peaceableness, meekness and kindness can master all violence. The world will be ours as soon as ever a sufficient number of men with purity of heart, with strength, and with perseverance, think and live out the thoughts of love and truth, of meekness and peaceableness." *

What to Do When There Is No Choice

I said that there were usually any number of things we could do to adjust ourselves to the world and the life around, but sometimes there seems to be no choice. I was in such a position recently.

It was during a flight over Africa in a foreign plane. We had put down for refueling, and my wife and I went into the tiny air terminal for refreshments. Sitting at a nearby table was the crew. These men were not only eating, they were also drinking generously of wine on this hot night. It seemed to me that they were soon glowing, and with carefree good humor their voices had become astonishingly loud. My wife and I agreed that the line was probably changing crews here and that these fellows had a right to celebrate. But when the call came for passengers and crew, who should lead off but our captain with his tie slightly off side on his shirt.

We got into the plane. The air was suffocating. The night was dead calm. The motors broke the silence like

* From *Memoirs of Childhood and Youth* (New York: The Macmillan Company, 1949).

ominous jungle drums. We left the field in a perfect takeoff. But a few moments after we were airborne, the motors seemed suddenly to cough, and for an instant we had that "sinking feeling." I looked at my wife. As our eyes met and she seemed to ask, "Is this regular?" the motors picked up and we were again flying smooth as a bullet.

She said, "What do you think?"

It was a good question. What would you have done in a case like this? Would you have rapped at the cabin door and said, "Fellows, you'd better let me out!"

The only thing we could do, the most realistic thing, was to exercise our will to believe that the crew knew what they were doing. It might not have looked that way to us. Perhaps they should have been a bit more careful in "changing the blowers." But we settled back and enjoyed the stars and the night and the good, fresh breeze as the air conditioners did their job.

The world is often like that. The flight through life often makes us wish we might have more of a command over the controls. There are times in everyone's life when he simply must depend upon another for his own destiny and his own fate. *Will to believe.*

Will to believe in the world and the life around, and fate and destiny will always be better to you. For behind every great achievement is the act of faith and behind every act of faith is God.

106

9. Test Cases in the Will to Believe in the World and the Life Around

SOMEONE IS ALWAYS ASKING ME, "HOW are you able to gain the confidence of a Penitente or a Hutterite or a Doukhobor or a Jehovah's Witness or a censer-swinging Maya-Quiche?"

There is only one answer. I will to believe that each one knows I am sincere in my research; that I am honestly trying to understand why he believes and worships as he does and am not intending to evaluate or judge or criticize what he has found or believes he has found. Need I tell him this? No, that would immediately belie what each of us instinctively recognizes. There is something mystical here. He feels what I know. He knows what I feel. My will to believe in him becomes his will to believe in me. You can prove this in test cases in your own life and you can observe it at work in others.

109

You Can Prove Your Will to Believe

Nowhere does this become clearer than among the Trappist monks. These men, who never speak, live deeply in a world where language is a thing of the heart. They do not need to ask. They know. Their knowledge of the world and the life around is deepened in the silences. Their will to believe becomes something apart from the spoken word.

I well remember my impressions during my first night in a Trappist monastery. I envied and feared these men. They had found something to which they could give complete and unquestioning loyalty and submission, but their unspoken thoughts and their willing and insular commitment to the Unseen were frightening. Within these walls, for thousands of days and nights, men fasted and prayed and mortified their bodies with a total disdain for attention or praise.

Now if we could develop the consciousness that as God rules in the life within He also governs in the world and the life around, our life would take on new meaning and a new attitude. Why not make a thirty-day test? Let us approach our work, our day-by-day contacts, our problems and our goals with a will to believe that the world and life around are harmonious and friendly, and see what changes take place.

Only You Can Remake Your World

No one can remake your world for you, if it wants remaking, except you yourself. No one can generalize and say that you ought to do this or that because another solved his problems in that particular way. We cannot afford to accept things just because they were good for someone else. The truth which inspires one person may destroy another. Each of us must *live through* to the solution of his problem.

The most important thing you can do for yourself in your own world, with your own destiny, with your own capacity and capabilities, is to will to believe that the life revolving around you is good. And as you exercise this will to believe, the world around you becomes good. It takes on the goodness generated by your faith.

Recently I visited the encampment of a trailer caravan. Five hundred trailers were parked for three days in a field on the outskirts of Guadalajara. Mexicans came from miles around to see how Americans live on wheels and to find out why they leave their beautiful homes to take to the road in *casas* no bigger than an adobe hut. They were no more amazed than I to learn that the majority of these cars were Cadillacs, that most of the travelers were retired, and that there were eight millionaires among the trekkers.

What interested me most during my interviews with a goodly number of these *"Americanos tipicos,"* as the Mexicans called them, was that each brought with him not only his home but his own little world. And this world was fashioned entirely by his attitude.

There was, for example, the man who sat in front of his trailer in the shade and told me, "I wouldn't go on another one of these trips if they paid me. We rush through the towns I want to see and we stay for three days where you can see everything in one afternoon. If I lag behind they call me a turtle and if I'd skin out ahead they'd call me a jack rabbit. It's no good."

Then there was the man who confided, "This is the greatest thing I've ever had a part in. Why, you know, everyone in this caravan is about the finest person you want to meet. It's a miracle how we all get along. We were stuck for three days because some bridges were washed out, and that was a real adventure. We feel like one big family, ambassadors of good will. It's the life!"

Yes, they carried their worlds with them. They created their worlds not in the cars they drove or in the trailers in which they ate and slept, but in their minds and hearts. And that, of course, is what ever seeker for Utopia has had to learn.

We Should Be Intellectually Honest

Should this will to believe in a world and a life around exclude an honest appraisal of our environment? Not at

112

all. If you sit in a burning house and say, "I will to believe that there is no fire," you will very likely be burned alive.

If you drink a bottle of poison and say, "I will to believe that this is a root beer float," you will probably suffer.

If you walk carelessly into a busy street and affirm, "I will to believe that I am a charmed pedestrian," the odds are that you will end up in the hospital or in jail or even in the morgue. It is assumed that we will to believe with reason. The closed mind usually destroys itself.

The Will to Believe Is Always the Strongest Choice

Let us say that you *are* caught in a burning house. Would it be better for you to say, "I will to believe that I shall escape?" or "I will to believe that I shall be burned alive?" Where does reason prompt you to throw the weight of your faith?

Or let us say that you are being compelled to drink poison. Would it be the better part of wisdom for you to say, "I will to believe that there is a Power which will not forsake me now"? Or "I will to believe that I shall surely die"?

And suppose you are forced to flee into a street of moving traffic, where there is no other escape? Why, then, you say, "I will to believe that God will help me now." But what if God doesn't help?

Then, to reiterate, we stand where Jesus stood in his

113

moment of deepest need, when He, too, seemed utterly forsaken and said as much upon the cross. We will to believe that, like Him, we shall also find the miracle beyond, which was His to find.

There are any number of things we can do as we try to adjust ourselves to the world and the life around us. We can resist, we can flee, we can submit, we can work to change the existing order. Whatever our decision, in any case, we should select our path according to the highest degree of our ability to choose, and then exercise a will to believe that this is right for us.

There are those who contend that the gospels do not contain any evidence of a belief in a common human brotherhood, and that Jesus never declared that *all* men are the children of God. But others read into both the gospels and Jesus' words the idea of universal fellowship and peace; it is up to us to will to believe which view is right for us.

Part III

THE WILL TO BELIEVE
IN THE WORLD
AND
THE LIFE BEYOND

10. Do We Live After Death?

I AM CONTINUALLY BEING ASKED, "DID you really talk with your sister who has been dead for twenty years?"

The question has been put to me with every possible inflection ever since the story was publicized several years ago,* and the desire to know exactly what happened is an indication of the deep-seated human curiosity about life after death.

The Allurement of the Unknown Is Universal

In fact, the reason more people go to church at Easter than at any other time of the year is for this very reason: the allurement of the unknown and the instinctive desire to learn what lies beyond. The wish to solve the riddle is

---

* From *They Have Found a Faith*, by Marcus Bach, copyright, 1946. Used by special permission of the publishers, The Bobbs-Merrill Company, Inc.

universal. Job put it into a phrase and we are still asking it, "If a man die shall he live again?"

Does Everyone Believe in Life After Death?

I took a poll in one of my university classes, inquiring of the 150 students how many of them had an active interest in or a curiosity about life after death. Every hand went up. Then I asked how many *believed* in life after death. I was due for a shock. Only 60 per cent were willing to say they did. I respected their candor.

These young people are decidedly more honest and outspoken in their views than I was at their age. For at that time in my life I was held in awe by ecclesiastical pronouncements and restrained by a symbolism of language, the meaning of which I did not comprehend, but to which I subscribed because the minister said I had to. The language may have had meaning for him. It had none for me.

Not so with students today. So when I asked them how many were convinced that there was something in life— the soul, the spirit, the psyche, the life essence, the ego, the "God stuff"—that would live on after death, only 60 per cent said they believed. But even the "doubting 40 per cent" said to me, "Now about that sister business. Was there really something to it or was it a trick?"

The incident in question happened in a spiritualistic seance. I am not a spiritualist. I never intend to become

120

one. I am not even a spiritualistic enthusiast. On the contrary, I think that some 97 per cent of what I have seen in "spiritualism" is hokus-pokus or self-delusion or mind-reading or chance or something that can or ought to be rather easily explained by any accredited member of the magicians' organization, the Linking Ring. But I am frank to say that after I have explained the 97 per cent, the residuum of three per cent has me baffled—and the "sister seance" belongs in the three per cent.

Let's Go to a Seance

It happened at Chesterfield, Indiana, where spiritual-istic conventions are held every summer and where investigators have maintained that phenomena occur for which there is no known law. I was frankly skeptical and after several days on the grounds had the feeling that in most cases the mediums played majestically upon my mental susceptibilities, leaving me quite as unconvinced as other mediums had during my years of seance sitting across the country.

There came a day, an early autumn afternoon, when I sat with three other men and three women in the base-ment room of a cottage for a materializing demonstration under the mediumship of one Fanchion Harwood. On this occasion I had permission to examine the room. We had entered by the outside cellar stairs. The door through which we had come was now locked. There was another door in the opposite corner of the room leading into another part of the basement. This was also locked. The walls were solid and so was the floor. The casement windows, locked, were covered by venetian blinds over which black velvet curtains had been drawn. The room was vividly lighted.

A black curtain was suspended in cyclorama fashion from one of the walls to create an enclosure some four feet in diameter and six feet high. This formed what mediums call the "cabinet." I pulled aside the curtain. There was a chair here with its back to the basement wall, and when I asked about this I was given the usual explanation.

"It is here that the materializing medium sits," said the woman whom I will call the "cabinet woman," Mrs. Harwood's assistant. "The cabinet shields the medium during the time the ectoplasmic force which builds the spirit forms is generated and assembled. This ectoplasm exudes from the medium's mouth and body in the nature of a gauzy, foggy, smoke-like substance from which spirits are formed by the spirit chemists."

"What about the lights?" I inquired.

"The bright lights will be turned off. Ectoplasm, with its quality of luminosity, shows up best in the dark or in semi-darkness. The seance will take place in a red light that will not detract from the materialized forms, and will be bright enough for you to discern one another all the while and to see me standing near the cabinet."

122

All of which sounded to me like the old routine.

Now there was a rap at the door and Mrs. Harwood was admitted. The door was then relocked.

Mrs. Harwood had been described as one who "wouldn't put anything over on you for the world," and that was exactly the impression this gentle and cordial middleaged woman gave me. She greeted us warmly and then, in a businesslike manner, stepped inside the "cabinet." Two of the women satisfied themselves that our medium had concealed nothing with which to perpetrate a hoax and, this done, the assistant took her place beside the drawn curtain. Mrs. Harwood now, so we were told, was going into a trance and we were requested to be in a reverent frame of mind.

We Receive Our Instructions

"I have these requests," said the cabinet woman. "Be sincere. Please do not speak among yourselves. If a spirit appears and indicates it wants to talk to you, if it calls you by name or motions to you to come, get up and speak to it. I only ask that you will please not touch the spirits."

"Why shouldn't we touch them?" I asked.

"There is a connection between the spirits and the medium. When you touch the spirit you are really touching the medium and disturbing the conditions of the trance. When Jesus appeared to Mary in the garden

123

after His resurrection He said, 'Touch me not, for I am not yet ascended to my Father.' "

I had further questions but kept them to myself. For I must admit that I have always been of the opinion that the success of a seance depends as much on those who form the "circle" as it does upon the medium. By this I mean that if there is "something to" spirit communication, it must surely be a highly sensitized technique. I have always been all for cooperating, but have also tried to be on guard against trickery or deception or whatever might be hidden under the tantalizing term "psychical demonstration."

So the assistant turned out the bright lights and gave the room over to the deep red glow of a gelatin-covered spotlight fixed to the wall directly over my shoulder. At my right sat a doctor of medicine from Texas, at my left a New York publisher of psychical literature. The others in our group of seven sat with us in a semi-circle, the room having sufficient light for them to be discernible to me at all times.

The "Phenomenon" Begins

After a few moments of silent waiting, the cabinet woman suggested that we sing a song. Someone started, "I heard the voice of Jesus say." We sang one verse and were about to begin another when a childlike voice spoke.

"How are you, everyone?" it asked. "I am Twilight."

124

At this everyone responded, "Hello, Twilight. How are you?"

"I'm just fine," said Twilight.

She was chatty. "I think this will be a good seance," she babbled. "Oh, a very good seance, I think for sure. It is a good circle. Oh, it's a good day for a seance. Nice and sunny. Atmospheric conditions have a lot to do with seances. When the atmosphere is heavy, it is hard for the spirits to manifest. Materialization is hard then. Oh, yes, it is. And we must have materializations! We just must have! All religions must have phenomen—how do you say it?"

Twilight giggled and I was annoyed, sure that this would be just another one of those things. Evidently Mrs. Harwood was a ventriloquist and this would merely be a duplication of what I had heard many times in many places.

Then a light flickered near the floor, a few feet from the cabinet and close to where the assistant stood. It was a luminous glow that came suddenly, tarried a moment, and faded slowly away. Twilight's chatter continued as the light loomed again. This time it mounted bright and shimmering and out of its smoky vortex a form began to appear. Something like shoulders, then a face was resolved as the luminescent stuff swirled into bodily form. Then a voice called one of the women in our circle by her first name. The woman got up, took a few steps, and said to the materialized form, "Yes, Mother?"

"How are you?" the "spirit" asked in a low whisper.

125

"I'm fine. Why didn't you bring Father with you?"

A man's voice said, "She did." And hovering suddenly beside the figure of the little old woman was the figure of a man. Then a third figure appeared, that of a young boy who whispered, "Mother, do you remember the walks we used to take?"

Mother said, "I surely do."

"Then," said the boy, "let's take one now!"

With this he took his mother's arm and promenaded across the room, so close to me that I pulled back my feet. Throughout all this Twilight interspersed her childish chatter, and there were whispers from the materialized forms, together with laughter, low and pleased.

Was This Deception?

I drew my attention from this "out-of-this-world" demonstration to analyze the possibilities of deception and fraud. The room, to which my eyes had become accustomed, was sufficiently lighted for me to see that there were no tricks which any reasonable member of a magicians' brotherhood would obviously discover. There was something different and unusual about this seance and, for the moment at least, deception was ruled out.

Once when the three figures brushed by, a voice cautioned, "It is getting very bright."

At this the cabinet woman came over and put another

126

thin sheet of gelatin over the spotlight behind my shoulder.

I was making mental notations of all that was happening—the hovering, swaying motion of the "spirits," the rhythm of life, in keeping with which was the rise and fall of the whispered voices, the suspended, throbbing motion of the moving figures. I watched and said to myself, "Now, let's figure this out." But I had come to no conclusion when, at the end of an hour, numerous "spirits" had materialized and dematerialized and most of the sitters in our circle had been called up. Nothing had happened to me.

A Mysterious Happening

Then the swirling ectoplasmic stuff rose from the floor to take on the form of a girl. And as she grew, she spoke in a whisper:

"Marc, dear . . . Marc, dear . . . Marc, dear."

I got up and walked toward her until we were some four feet apart.

I asked, "Who are you?"

"Don't you know me?"

"No, I don't know you. Who are you?"

She said, "Paula."

Some twenty years ago my sister Paula had died at the age of twenty-three. Her child, Janette, had died shortly before her own passing. These deaths had been among the deep sorrows in our family, but time and travel had reduced them into forgetfulness. I had to confess that no medium or spirit or mind reader had plucked this name out of my mind because I had not once thought about Paula during this seance. I had, instead, been thinking about a friend of mine, a young man who had been killed not long before in a plane crash.

"How do I look?" the figure asked.

"You look fine," I replied.

What About Recognition?

The outline of the form and features resembled Paula, as I remembered her, sufficiently to make her recognizable at least. But then, the mind plays tricks and I am sure that her mention of other relatives who had died— and who sent "greetings"—helped more than this to draw me into a web of belief and credulity. The materialized form was like a "false front," a flat, two-dimensional body with a semblance of arms, clothed in a shadowy gray-white film. The face was typically mask-like. Paula used to wear her hair "page-boy style," and that is what the contour of this materialized "hair" was like. I would not be able to say whether the whispered voice resembled Paula's or not. I could not remember.

But this is what flashed through my mind. Could it have been possible for someone at Chesterfield—I had been there about a week—to have done some quick research on my family, and through a well-laid system of espionage to have come up with the facts about Paula's death and also Paula's description? It could be, though at three dollars for the seance someone was probably losing money!

But, let's say they did go to this trouble and get the facts; then what I saw before me must be a puppet, voiced by a ventriloquist and manipulated in a most clever fashion. So the thing for me to do would be to reach out and touch this figure and find out for myself what this ectoplasmic stuff was really like.

Questions and Answers About Life After Death

I moved closer. I stepped slightly to one side so that the red light would strike Paula's face more directly. We were about three feet apart. She was talking about life in the spirit world and asked whether I had any questions. I had many: Have you seen Jesus? What is heaven like? How do you measure time? Can you be everywhere at once? What are the first experiences of a soul after death?

She had answers. "No one has seen Jesus. He is in the philosophers' heaven."

"Heaven is like thought that is made alive."

"I do not think about time."

"Thought can be everywhere at once."

129

"Death is like waking from a sleep. If the death is violent, the awaking is troubled. If death is quiet, the awaking is quiet. It is like that."

Then a thought came to me. "Paula," I said, "do you remember the catechism we kids learned at home?"

"Of course."

"What is the first question in that catechism?"
The answer came at once. " 'What is your chief comfort in life and in death?' "

"Go on," I urged.

" 'That I, with body and soul, both in life and in death am not my own . . .' " She interrupted herself to say, "Here where we are the words have a greater meaning."

Then quickly, breathlessly, she assured me that serving God means personal development. Death, she insisted, was not a violent result of sin. It had no sting. It was neither friend nor enemy. It was simply part of life, part of the divine purpose, and whoever tried to solve that purpose would find it had no beginning and no end. Several times she asked anxiously, "Do you understand? Is that clear?"

The whispering grew fainter. "I can stay no longer. I must go now."

"Paula," I urged, "one more thing. Will you put your arms around me?"

She said, "I'll give you a kiss. Come close."

"You come close." I said. I wanted her to come nearer

130

the red light. She did. Her face was luminous, seemingly transparent, and without depth.

I leaned forward and lowered my head. Something like arms went around my neck. Something soft and flaxen brushed my forehead; it was only a slight sensation, almost physically unfelt. Then Paula or whatever it was de-materialized into the floor and disappeared.

I walked back to my chair and sat down.

"Was that all right?" Twilight was asking. "What do you think?"

I did not reply.

I did not know what to think.

The doctor leaned over and whispered, "What do you make of it?"

I had no answer.

We waited until the bright lights were turned on and the cabinet woman called to Mrs. Harwood, "Are you all right?" There was a stirring inside the curtain and in a moment the medium appeared. Either by design or circumstances, she gave the impression of being completely exhausted. I shook hands with her and told her frankly that this particular seance had aspects which could not be easily explained or quickly dismissed.

She agreed.

11. Belief in Life After Death Is an Act of Faith

IT HAS BEEN A PRINCIPLE WITH THOSE who have come to terms with life that we grow mentally and spiritually as the result of reflection.

As I thought about my seance experience it seemed to me that an infinitely good destiny hung over life—over everyone's life. I felt with a great sense of confidence that underneath all of life's adventures were "the everlasting arms," the creative force of the universe, and that this force was reflected in me as the very essence of life; not in me only, but in all living things.

I felt that this present life and the life beyond were *one* life and that what we call death is but the *door* from life to life. I seemed to know with a great conviction that eternity was actually a part of the here and now.

The seance had set the stage or created the conditions for this awareness, but there was a more positive and significant element in the experience, namely, a *will to believe*. This was the result of a conscious act on my part. It could have been induced under any of a number of circumstances, and certainly can and has come to many people without the motivation of a seance. It happens whenever and wherever a person takes time out to consider his life in the light of his relationship with God.

Quiet Reflection Deepens Our Will to Believe

Quiet reflection is the secret. Let a man steal a few moments out of his busy rush and chances are he will come nearer to God and truth through personal meditation than he will by listening to a year of sermons. We desperately need to be reflective. In order to *know*, we must stop our *go*. That is how a will to believe is born—out of reflection and through a conscious effort.

It Is an Act of Faith

The belief in life after death is strictly an act of faith. We believe because we will to believe. And we should will to believe it because then this present life takes on new meaning. We arrive at a new appraisal in our sense of values, a new dimension, a true perspective.

136

Belief in life after death helps us to create our highest possible type of society. When we exercise a will to believe in a world and a life beyond, we realize that what we hold in common with God we also hold in common with all men.

Here Is One Area in Which We Can All Agree

We may never be able to agree sociologically. We shall probably always be arguing as to which race is superior, white, black, yellow, brown, or red.

We may never agree psychologically on our attitudes, customs or tastes. We may not be able to reach a mutual understanding as to where a man should live, what he should eat or what he should wear.

We may never agree economically on the matter of possessions, or educationally on the matter of knowledge.

We may never agree theologically. Not all Catholics will become Protestants or all Protestants, Catholics; nor will all non-Christians become Christians, no matter how ambitious anyone's missionary efforts may be.

There is but one area in which we can all agree: whatever is the essence of life in one man is the essence of life in all men. Add to this a will to believe that this essence of life is God in us, and that it is immortal, and then this present life in all its relationships will take on a new meaning.

137

The Will to Believe Can Remake Your World, but It Requires Effort

Ten per cent of our people are mentally ill. Much of this is due to a limited perspective and the idea that this mortal, physical life is all there is to life, that we had better, by all means, squeeze out of these fleeting years every enjoyment we possibly can. "We'll be a long time dead," as the saying goes. We keep telling ourselves, "You had better make all the money you can and have all the fun you can and be the most popular and prominent person you can, because you certainly 'can't take it with you.'"

We have tried for a long time to spiritualize the secular life, but there is good evidence that in actuality we have secularized the spiritual life until many religionists themselves are hinting that we had better "eat, drink and be merry and successful," because tomorrow we die. Others say that we are all becoming Schlemihls—like Peter Schlemihl, that is, the man who had no shadow because he had sold it to the devil for the purse that would never run dry. And that is why we are mentally ill.

Here Is How We Can Get a New Outlook on this Present Life

Now, let us assume that we develop the will to believe that these few years are *not* all there is to life. Let us

138

say we will to believe unequivocally that this life is part of a larger life. What kind of a larger life? I do not know. No one knows. It is speculative. But since we came into this physical life completely unfamiliar with what awaited us here, yet learned to live it, so, too, we can believe that in the "life to come" we shall learn to live in the kind of world and under the kind of conditions that await us there.

Our Will to Believe Is Often Opposed by an Inner Will NOT to Believe

I said we can believe it. I should have said we can *will* to believe it, for that is the secret. And the greater secret is that this will to believe does not come easily; it requires effort. It requires a volitional act. The trouble with most of us, and the trouble with institutionalized religion, is that it has always hinted that belief comes easily. It doesn't.

For a reason never fully explained, not even by Paul, and not considered as needing explanation by Jesus, we are in constant danger of being robbed of our will to believe by an opposing will to disbelieve. It may be that without warfare of this kind one never wins a victory. It may be that our will to disbelieve is the foil which sharpens our will *to* believe. However that may be, the will to believe in a world and a life beyond this life requires constant effort on our part.

139

Some religious enthusiasts disagree. They say belief is easy, natural, "no trick at all." They say, "How dare you imply that life after death is speculative or hypothetical? Didn't Jesus rise from the dead? Didn't He tell us that because He lives we shall live also? Don't you believe your Bible?"

I do. But I believe my Bible because I will to believe it. Had I been present when Jesus appeared after His resurrection, I would very likely have believed just as much—and just as little—as the disciples believed. In other words, I would have believed just as much and just as little as the disciples' *will to believe* persuaded them to accept as truth, concerning what they saw and heard.

Do the Scriptures Prove the Scriptures?

I attended an Amadiyyah service, the group which believes that Jesus did not die upon the cross, but that He merely lost consciousness and was taken from the cross and spirited away by His disciples. They believe, among other things, that He went to India with His gospel message and died there. But what was stressed most emphatically at this service was that the Koran, the Moslem scripture, is true because the Koran says it is true. The speaker announced that all other scriptures, the Bible included, would have to be judged by the Koran. And that is precisely what every ardent follower says of *his* holy book. What he ought honestly to say is that what each reads in his scripture is true for him because he wills to believe it.

How to Live with Your Beliefs

I will to believe that Jesus rose from the dead. I also will to believe that two disciples were walking to Emmaus, and that they looked up and saw a third figure walking with them. They invited Him into the house and He sat with them at the table. He broke bread and vanished from their sight. Can I prove it? No. Can anyone prove it? No. Does the fact that it is recorded in the Bible prove it? No. The Bible does not prove it; it simply reports it. I believe because I will to believe. That is how I accept the transfiguration, the appearance in the garden, the incident of the Upper Room, and everything else that has to do with a world and a life beyond this life.

I will to believe in a world and a life beyond because it establishes a devotion to a higher good and answers in faith the universal questing of the essence of life within me.

It is in such terms, rather than in terms of an obsolescent clash between fundamentalism and modernism, or between Biblical literalism and Biblical liberalism, that the problem of life after death must be posed. "Does a man have the will to believe it?"—that is the question. Reason and revelation convince some men that the soul of man is immortal, and occasionally scientists confirm the conviction, but within the process, admittedly or not, is the will to believe. And it seems to me that the very desire on the part of humankind to will to believe it admits no other conclusion than that a spiritual relationship with God exists, and that according to man's very nature, man is immortal.

"But," you might well ask, "isn't this being highly unscientific? What does science have to say about heaven and the life beyond?"

Out Beyond Our Knowing Is the Great Unkown

Astronomer J. Hugh Pruett recently made an interesting and candid observation, "Perhaps it is unfortunate that 'the heavens' and 'Heaven' are terms so much alike in sound but so different in meaning. Many ancient peoples considered this firmament to be a solid dividing surface. Below it birds flew and clouds floated; above it was the abode of the Deity and the spirits of the blessed. Heaven to them was definitely a material place above the world. . . . The study of astronomy has never been able to give any light on the location of 'Heaven.' No telescope has detected such a place. Such discussions belong mostly in the realm of philosophy and religion. Astronomy is primarily concerned with material locations and actions, although the wonder aroused may lead to extremely interesting speculations."

142

When physicist Arthur H. Compton expressed his views on immortality in his article "Death, or Life Eternal?" * he said, "A man trained in the school of science has a deep-seated reluctance to present evidence which can only be considered as suggestive. Yet many who profess to speak for science have drawn the definite conclusion that death is the end of all. It takes but little investigation to find that this faith in the completeness of physical death is usually based upon an uncritical acceptance of a common-sense realism, similar to that which accepts a brick as the hard, heavy, red object that can be held in the hands.

"Just as a more careful examination shows the brick to consist of a group of molecules, atoms, and electrons —a complex system of electrical fields wholly different from the common-sense picture—so the 'obviousness' of death is found to disappear when more closely studied. Though it is true that science presents no weighty evidence for life eternal, it is only fair to point out also that science has found no cogent reason for supposing that what is of importance in a man can be buried in a grave. The truth is that science cannot supply a definite answer to this question."

It would be well if we held religious concepts as discreetly as scientists hold their theories. They do not insist that they have reached the ultimate answer. They

---

* Arthur H. Compton, *The Freedom of Man* (New Haven: Yale University Press, 1935).

143

do not insist that the last word has been spoken in any given field. Out beyond their knowing is the great and challenging Unknown, and they are frank enough to admit that this is the case.

So my students say to me, "You really believe that there is a world and a life beyond this life?"

"Yes."

"Can you prove it?"

"No, I cannot prove it."

"Then how can you believe it?"

"I will to believe it."

"Isn't this unscientific?"

"No more unscientific than not to believe it."

"But why do you will to believe it?"

And I tell them again that when we believe that we are co-workers and partners with God in a world that has dimensions beyond this life, we are as of now already co-workers and partners with Him in this present world—and that the two worlds and the two lives are one.

12. The Life to Come and Our Will to Live

WHEN POPE PIUS XII WAS SERIOUSLY
ill, a friend of mine asked a pertinent question. "Why,"
he wanted to know, "does everyone pray that Pius will
recover? Even Protestants joined in prayer for him.
Why shouldn't the Pope of all people be happy to die
and eager to go to heaven? Why all this praying and
desperate hanging on to life?"

It was a relevant question and could have been answered in the obvious way: Catholics wanted Pius XII
to live because they loved him and felt that they needed
him. He was their leader, a Pope of peace and a man
for the times.

Protestants prayed for his recovery out of a common
sympathy and Christian charity. Perhaps they also
hoped thereby to close the gap in the divided house of

147

Christendom. They saw here a personal and a human situation in which they sincerely wished to join in a spirit of brotherhood. And so on. But it was still a thought-provoking question: why all this desperate attempt on the part of professing Christians to hang on to life?

"My friends, what think ye?" cried Nietzsche. "Will ye not, like me, say unto death: 'Was *that*—life? For the sake of Zarathustra, well, once more!' "

In Our Will to Live We Stand on Common Ground

Come now, let's agree. Most Christians are as reluctant to let go of this present life as are most non-Christians. Few indeed, Christian or not, believer or non-believer, make their demise as did actor Tom Moore, who died at seventy-one. More than a month after his illness had been diagnosed as malignant cancer he took a starring role in a television play. Then he returned to his bed and predicted almost to the day when he would die. His last words were, "I certainly will know how to play a death scene after this."

It is said that Thoreau, during his last moments, was asked, "Have you made your peace with God?"

"I have never quarreled with Him," he said.

A friend of mine who spent most of his life vagabonding around the globe developed an incorrigible

148

sense of humor. He could not bring himself to take seriously the everlasting bickering between individuals or nations. He said he had it on inner authority—by which he meant faith, not facts—that life was but an entr'acte in the great drama of existence, a way station between many lives.

As he lay near death, the physician, a close companion, sighed and said, "Well, old man, it will be just like taking another trip. You always like to travel."

"True," was the reply. "And I always like to travel light."

He had what many mature minds eventually disclose: an easy-going tendency about the Unknown. There is a submerged intelligence that, if given a chance, instinctively raises our will to believe to a philosophical height, above any "logic-chopping" or argumentative ritual, and says, "Here is a faith to live by."

That is why reflective people meet death serenely. They have willed to believe, they *know,* that there is that Something, that Someone within who is no stranger to the world and the life beyond.

Men may joke about death or write their own humorous epitaphs as an escape from an inner fear about dying, but they may also do so because they intuitively know that there is no death; there is only change and transition, that mysterious interval, that catching of the breath between life and life.

But Life Is Always Precious

Almost invariably, the vaunted talk about the beauty of heaven does not keep the most sanctimonious from sending out a frantic call to the specialists! Those who most vociferously condemn the allurements of this material world are among the most reluctant to take a chance on the City Foursquare. It is a well-publicized secret that those who most ambitiously promote others into heaven want for themselves the longest possible duration of this present sojourn.

It has well been said, "If heaven is really as terrific as some folks say, it must be hell for them to stay around here so long."

So what happens to our vaunted will to believe in a world and a life beyond? Is it pure fabrication, a wishful thought without substance, a crutch and an illusion? Are we simply fictionizing when we will to believe that there is something within us that never dies?

No. It is a case of our will to believe in a spirit world being confronted by an equally instinctive *will to live* in this physical world. One does not cancel out the other. One does not minimize or invalidate the other. It is not even a paradox. The physical self wills to live, and the psychical self also wills to live, and a choice between them can be made only at the cost of a specific will. Why this is so, I do not know. But it is not true that because a man evidences a strong will to live he has doubts about the world and the life beyond. It is simply

150

"in the nature of things" for all of us to wish instinctively to live. And it is equally true that as we grow older we instinctively think of death less and less as an enemy and more and more as a friend.

Metaphysicist W. G. Langworthy Taylor puts it this way, "The man who has struggled up in the world from humble beginnings to knowledge, competence, and influence has already passed many a barrier more forbidding than death. He is used to dying and welcomes each death as a promotion. It is, after all, a sort of business, this advance from environment to environment, and becomes a matter of course, a second nature." *

How One Person Viewed the World and the Life Beyond

A speaker in one of my university classes, a Theosophist, put the thought into rather beautiful and graphic terms when he said, "I remember visiting Aunt Jenny. Hers was as lovely a disposition and character as I have ever known. She was an invalid for many years but her interest was always in people and in how she might help others and in how she might remember to do the little thoughtful things that were so typical of her nature. She once told me, 'As I lie here in my bed, I often take a long and beautiful walk.'

" 'Where do you walk, Aunt Jenny?'

---

* W. G. Langworthy Taylor, *Immortality* (Boston: Bruce Humphries, Inc., 1937). Reprinted by permission.

" 'Into a lovely garden where God is walking, too. And, do you know, I keep walking deeper and deeper into that garden with Him.'

"And that is what Aunt Jenny taught me about death. We walk into the garden with God and there comes a day when our will to be there with Him out-reaches our will to be with those we love on earth. That, it seems to me, is how Nature intended death to be."

Every One of Life's Experiences Is Interesting and Important

When did you last hear a sermon on immortality, and where do you go to have your questions on the subject of life after death sympathetically answered? Or do you agree with Lin Yutang, who asserted, "Too much preoccupation with immortality has something pathological about it."

But even this forthright philosopher arrived at a basic conclusion: "Many people have substituted for this personal immortality, immortality of other kinds, much more convincing, the immortality of the race, and the immortality of work and influence. It is sufficient that when we die, the work we leave behind us continues to influence others and play a part, however small, in the life of the community in which live. We can pluck the flower and throw its petals to the ground, and yet its subtle fragrance remains in the air." *

---

* From *The Importance of Living*, p. 399.

152

An earlier philosopher had a different idea. Emmanuel Kant hinted that the death of the body might actually be the beginning of a new life in which the mind, no longer restricted by its need for recording physical sensations, could now reflect unimpeded upon the deeper impressions of the spiritual life.

Innumerable times, after I have spoken on "My Adventures in Spiritualism," someone says to me, "I want to tell you about a psychic experience I had," or "Would you mind if I told you my views on the life to come?" or "Something happened to me that I simply can't explain. I've just got to tell somebody about it." These discourses are frequently prefaced by the confession, "You know, I wouldn't dare talk to my minister about this!"

I assure them that I am not a spiritualist. But I also assure them that I am interested in their adventures. And because every one of life's experiences is interesting and important, I listen. So they tell me the story of a materialization, or spirit communication, or some other phenomena, always showing a heartfelt desire to know whether or not the dead really live.

It is this craving for light and this desire for some kind of answer that prompt many people to attend spiritualistic seances and to seek out purported mediums. Spiritualism is traditional religion's unpaid bill. People are going to look for answers in their spiritual questing even if it means going off the beaten path to do it.

153

In this religiously intensified age man feels both courageous and free to find "truth" wherever truth is found. You will not frighten him from the quest about life after death with isolated Scripture texts, not even with Paul's admonition to the Romans, "Stay away from those who have familiar spirits."

I once met a man at a seance who said, "My preacher warned me that I'd go to hell if I came here. He told me that this kind of investigation is forbidden by the Bible. 'But, Preacher,' I said, 'if we take that portion of the Bible literally then what are we going to do with a passage that says, "Lay not up treasures on earth," or "Sell all that you have and give it to the poor?" ' "

This is the kind of age in which we are living, and every thoughtful minister and priest knows that the members of his congregation are literally in the pulpit with him, looking over his shoulder at the printed word, reading his mind, testing his sayings, and studying his life.

Do We Need Proof in Order to Believe?

One evening a man said to me, "Would you mind making an appointment with a reputable medium so that my wife can have a seance arranged? Three years ago our only son, seventeen, commited suicide. It was a terrible thing and my wife has never gotten over the shock of it. What worries her most is that she thinks Tom is being continually punished in hell for what he

154

did. Now, if she could go to a seance and if Tom could be contacted, that would be the greatest thing that could possibly happen."

I told him regretfully that much as I would like to comply with his request, I felt it would be unwise for me to do so.

I said, "I am not convinced about the reliability of what happens at these seances. It might, as you say, be the greatest thing that could possibly happen. It might also be the most disillusioning thing that could happen. It might be fraudulent."

Some weeks later I received a letter from this man's wife. She reported that since I had been reluctant to recommend a medium, she had gone forward on her own and made an appointment for the seance. In one of the most considerate and straight-forward letters that I have ever received in this connection, this mother wrote me that she had seen and spoken to her son, had put test questions to him, was fully convinced the seance was genuine, and was sure beyond any doubt that God had mercifully received her son and that "Tom lives."

But this kind of "evidence" was not at all needed by a mother who lost two sons during the war. She simply said, "I believe they live with God, therefore I know."

In the well-remembered *Go Down Death,* James Weldon Johnson, speaking of "Sister Caroline" says,

> While we were watching 'round her bed,
> She turned her eyes and looked away,

155

> She saw what we couldn't see;
> She saw Old Death. She saw Old Death
> Coming like a falling star.
> But Death didn't frighten Sister Caroline;
> He looked to her like a welcome friend.
> And she whispered to us: I'm going home.
> And she smiled and closed her eyes.*

Of course, to many people the problem of the *will to believe* has become equivalent to the question as to whether or not a thing can be proved. A dangerous misconception of metaphysics is here at stake, for it is begging the question to say that something which cannot be proved does not exist. "Faith is the substance of things *hoped* for; the *evidence* of things not seen." The world is full of attitudes built upon faith; and, as we have been saying, every ideal, every hope, every wish, every forward-moving step in human relations, and the rise of human culture rests upon a will to believe.

Do Not Let Your Want of Proof Impede Your Will to Believe

Creation is an eternal process and the object created is organically interrelated with its Creator. Can this be proved? No. It is an apprehension, a theory, a supposition. But by believing it we rise in the level of life. I

---

* From "Go Down Death" in *God's Trombones* (New York: The Viking Press, 1927).

156

do not mean by this that what we intuitively feel is more valid than what natural knowledge or research demonstrates, but neither should our want of proof impede our will to believe.

Let us never forget that religion for most people implies immortality. When we talk about salvation we usually mean life after death. Every living religion and most forgotten religions include the after-life in some form among their major concepts, so deep-seated and earnest is this longing in the human heart.

Immortality is the climax of religion itself, and ever since man's first faint dawn of faith he has had his rites, his rituals, his philosophy of the continuity of spiritual existence, and his theories about the resurrection of the body.

How has this been perpetuated and sustained? On the basis of experience, reason, or law? No. It is the result of faith: faith in an idea intellectually conceived and spiritually confirmed. In other words, a will to believe in the world and the life beyond.

157

13. Let's Look at the Record

Everyone who has been interested in the techniques of spirit communicaton has found rather strong support in several important publications. Albert Payson Terhune's *Across the Line* cannot be taken lightly.

No less a scholar than Dr. Joseph R. Sizoo of the Collegiate Church of St. Nicholas consented to write the foreword, which said, "The human heart has always rebelled against the silence of death. . . . Here is the record of one who makes the great affirmation that it (communication) is not only possible, but that it has been experienced. This is not the first voice that has protested against the silence of death and cried out exultantly, 'I have heard and I have seen.' God has given to the spirtually sensitive to lift the curtain for us and let in the light." *

Current Interest in Life After Death Is Widespread

Steward Edward White in *The Betty Book*, Casper Yost in *Patience Worth*, and Whitley in *Ministry of the*

---

* From the book *Across the Line*, by Albert Payson Terhune. Copyright, 1945, by Anice Terhune; published by E. P. Dutton & Co., Inc.

161

Unseen—to say nothing of such writers as Sir Oliver Lodge, A. Conan Doyle and Arthur Chambers—are all in support, not only of a life beyond, but of intercommunication with the dead. Recently several important newcomers to the field have added their testimonies: Sherwood Eddy, *You Will Survive After Death;* James Crenshaw, *Telephone Between Worlds;* Horace Westwood, *There Is a Psychic World.*

E. Katherine Bates has a suggestion for those who want to "make contact." She says, "Give a few minutes every day when you are quite peaceful and quite alone, to concentrate your mind on the one you wish to speak to. Think of him or her as simply as possible. . . call them by name. . . speak to them as if they were as close to you as I fully believe they are . . . if you persevere, some realization of the presence of the beloved one will come to you, so undeniable and so convincing to your own consciousness that a whole college of philosophers or scientists will not be able to persuade you that the one you loved and lost was not in close touch with you." *

There Is Agreement About Life after Death

Researchers and investigators who have done significant work in the psychical field are in complete agreement on two counts. They all believe that "the dead live" and they all are outspoken in their conclusion that there

---

* E. Katherine Bates, *Do the Dead Depart?* (New York: The McBride Co., Inc., 1929).

is a great amount of trickery employed among commercial mediums. Hereward Carrington, Camille Flammarion, Hamlin Garland, among the best of the students of psychical research, say, in effect, "Be wary when you go to a seance!"

Carrington, after more than fifty years of investigation of spiritualistic phenomena, was compelled to say, "There is scarcely a medium who has not, at one time or another, been exposed in the grossest kind of fraud." But then he added, "I do not wish it to be understood that I hereby relegate the whole evidence of the supernormal to the wastebasket. That is precisely what I do *not* wish to do. It is because I believe that there do exist certain phenomena, the explanations for which have not yet been found, that I think it necessary to distinguish these from the fraudulent marvels so commonly produced." *

That is my conclusion. I do not know why even reputable mediums frequently resort to deception, but they do. It may be that they sometimes "lose their touch" and try to simulate actual phenomena by artificial devices. It is, at best, difficult to understand; as difficult as it is to understand why ministers and priests occasionally preach things which they do not truly believe, and as difficult to explain as why parents are not always completely honest in answering the questions of their

---

* Hereward Carrington, *The Psychical Phenomenon of Spiritualism.* Used by permission of Dodd, Mead & Co., Inc.

children. Mediums are certainly not above suspicion, and I must admit that, like Carrington, I have sat in on many a fraudulent seance.

The Power of Mind over Mind

So, frankly, I often ask myself the same question that others are continually asking me, "Now, what do you think really happened during that Paula seance?"

The query was never put to me more bluntly than one day when a young man walked into my office. He was a psychiatrist, Dr. John Middents, and he had read my account of the Paula incident.

"Do you want to know what happened in that seance?" he challenged. "You were hypnotized."

"Could be," I replied.

"Have you ever been hypnotized?"

"Not that I know of!"

"Mind if I hypnotize you?"

"No."

That evening a small group of friends and I gathered for the hypnotic session. Dr. Middents asked me to sit in a comfortable chair and concentrate on the hypnotic device, the end of a pencil which he held some three or four feet from my eyes.

I concentrated.

So far as I can determine, I was consciously cooperating with Dr. Middents in the procedure. I was sincerely trying to submit to his inducement of: "Sleep . . . sleep . . . sleep . . ." and was ready to go along with him in his, "You are feeling drowsy . . . drowsy . . . drowsy . . . ," but nothing happened to me. Perhaps I was subconsciously resisting him. Be that as it may, at the end of perhaps five minutes he said, "You don't hypnotize. Or perhaps I'm losing my touch. Let me try someone else."

A student by the name of Don, a junior in the university, said that hypnotism would suit him just fine and he took my place in the chair.

At the end of perhaps five minutes, Dr. Middents had Don in a lovely hypnotic sleep. While Don was sleeping, Dr. Middents gave him this post-hypnotic instruction: "Soon you will awaken and you will feel very rested. Everything will be just as it was before you went to sleep, with one exception. You will not be able to recognize the letter 'e' until tomorrow morning at nine o'clock."

This was about ten o'clock in the evening. Then he brought the student out of the hypnotic state.

We sat talking together after that and during the conversation I casually asked Don how to spell "eat." He promptly replied, "A—t."

"That's not right," I said. "Try it again."

"A—t," he answered, annoyed.

I then asked him how he spelled his girl friend's name, which happened to be Collister.

165

He spelled it, "C—o—l—l—i—s—t—r."

"Write it down for me," I suggested.

He did. He wrote it without the "e."

At nine-thirty the following morning Don came into my office, grinning from ear to ear.

"Do I feel like a chump!" he exclaimed. "I had an eight-thirty class, and look at my notebook!"

The lecture notes he had taken from eight-thirty until nine were "e"-less. At nine o'clock his "e" came back!

There Is a Close Relationship Between Hypnotism and Seance "Phenomena"

I mention this by way of preface to what happened several nights later. Dr. Middents, still pursuing his thesis that I had been hypnotized during the Chesterfield seance, suggested another meeting. On this occasion, in the presence of five of us who were interested in the experiment, he again hypnotized the student. This time, during the hypnotic sleep, he said, "Don, your grandmother is in the room."

Don shook his head. "Gran'ma's dead."

"She's in the room," Dr. Middents insisted. "Do you see her?"

"No, I don't see her."

"She is here. Open your eyes and look at her."

Don opened his eyes. After an instant of staring

starkly into space, a smile crossed his face and he said, "How are you, Gran'ma?"

"What's Gran'ma wearing?" I asked.

"She's wearing a long black dress with buttons all down the front and she's got her hair fixed on the top of her head. How are you, Gran'ma?"

It was a convincing demonstration of the close relationship between what might happen in a seance room and what happens under hypnosis. Perhaps I should have had the will to believe that this fully explained the Paula seance! But I didn't. The close similarity did not invalidate what I felt had happened at the Chesterfield meeting nor did it convince me that I might have been hypnotized in the seance room when it was seemingly impossible for me to be hypnotized, willingly, out of the seance room.

Be that as it may, I am ready to admit that the possibility of hypnotism playing a part in so-called spiritualistic phenomena certainly exists, and I never go to a seance without keeping this possibility in mind and guarding against it.

14. Your Will to Believe and the Mystery of the Unknown

I<small>F</small>, <small>WHILE YOU ARE SITTING QUIETLY IN</small> your room, someone comes in with the announcement, "This room is full of music," you might charitably agree by saying, "That's right. All we need is a radio to prove it."

You might even go along with the contention that, "This room is full of pictures," and agree that a TV set would prove or disprove that.

But if you were told, "This room is full of spirit voices!" you would perhaps be less inclined to agree. You might, however, be willing to bring in a medium—the necessary "receiving set"—to convince you that spirit voices and spirit presences do or do not exist.

I asked an electronics engineer the obvious question, "Do radio and television waves exist in the room even though there are no receiving sets present, or do the sets bring them in?"

He replied, "I'll answer that with an even older question. If a tree falls in the forest and there is no one present to hear it crash, was there a sound to its falling?"

That is what spiritualists say about spirit voices and spirit presences. "If there is a spirit vibration in a room and there is no person there to receive it, does the vibration exist?"

Why Spirit Communication?

And what is the purpose of spirit communication? What's the good of it? To this spiritualists reply, "Why do you listen to radio news reports? To keep in touch with your world. You should listen to spirit voices in order to keep in touch with the world to come."

It has always seemed to me that most of the so-called spirit communications amounted to little more than drivel. I have attended many a seance where a great deal of time and effort and technique were expended to "make contact," and then when a voice came through it said, "Granny sends love," or "The flowers over here are very sweet," or "We aren't bothered by the price of butter and coffee the way you are!" There may be more importance in these pronouncements than I realized, but they hardly seemed momentous to me.

Spiritualists, who always have an answer, informed

172

me that "A departed soul is not endowed with sudden omniscience. There is none of this being changed in the twinkling of an eye. If Granny and flowers and butter and coffee were important to folks here, they are still important to folks when they have crossed over. Furthermore, if you are suddenly called upon to speak, over a microphone, let's say, how clever or how erudite are you? It is that way with the spirits of the departed. Life over there is progressive, but it is also reflective of the life lived here and of the interests and attitudes of people while they inhabited the physical plane. If a medium contacts a scientist he talks like a scientist, and if a medium contacts a gossip he talks like a gossip."

Which reminds me that I once attended a trumpet seance in which the spirit of Professor William James was purportedly contacted. All I can say about that experience is that either the spiritualist was himself a reincarnation of the late psychologist or it really *was* William James. It was that convincing.

What Should Be Our Attitude Toward Modern Psychical Phenomena?

Now, of course, most Christians have the will to believe in the "spiritistic" happenings recorded in the Bible. They may not like the term *spiritistic*, but that is merely a semantic difficulty. Why do they believe that such phenomena occurred in Biblical times but do not

173

happen today? They either have the will to believe that that was a special dispensation, or that the Biblical writers and observers were infallible, or that God does things in His own way and in His own time and always leaves some undeniable evidence of His manifestations. They may say that He left this evidence in Biblical times but does not leave it today. But actually, they believe what they believe because of their will to believe it.

Is There a Final Word?

Modern man's will to believe, however, need not take up any dogmatic attitude or irreconcilable position in regard to the mystery of the Unknown. It may—in fact, it should—recognize the possibility of many avenues of belief and the many roads that wind in and out of belief and unbelief. It should take into account many experiences, some proved to a degree, some imagined, even some that have been deliberately staged, and find within all of them a hint of man's everlasting quest and the insatiable longing to know what to think and what to believe about the world and the life beyond.

Remembering how long humanity has searched and probed for light upon this puzzling path, how from the ageless rituals for the dead to the very thought of one's own passing, man has reflected on his immortal destiny, who dares to say, "I have the final word?" It is my will to believe that steps in to reconcile *this* world with *that* world, and assures me that what we call death is but an opening door from life to life.

"But," you say, "you may be wrong."

I can only answer, "Yes—and I may be right."

My mother, whose will to believe in life after death needed no telltale evidence, had always warned me to "stay away from puppet shows and mediums; both are of the devil." But some months after the Chesterfield seance I casually remarked to her, "I saw Paula the other day."

She asked, "Paula . . . who?"

"Our Paula."

Then I told her the story. She listened intently and, to my surprise, asked quietly, "Did she look like Paula? Did you recognize her? Did she say anything more?"

My dad, who had been listening and who had taken many a thoughtful drag at his cigar, spoke up.

"Don't tell me," he exclaimed to my mother, "that you put any stock in this story!"

To which my mother replied, "In a day of radio and atom bombs, who can say what will happen next?"

But she immediately qualified this by saying:

"For the Christian There Is Always Christ"

And when she said that, she was speaking for all Christendom with its many and varied divisions; she

175

was testifying for every Christian who has the will to believe.

The will to believe what? That the individual has free access to the Spirit of Christ and needs no mediumistic middleman to prove or affirm the survival of personal consciousness. The verdict of the Christian faith so far as immortality is concerned has been clearly stated, "He died and rose again and because He lives we, too, shall live."

That is why the Christian so often says, "It is not *what* I believe, but Whom!"

This is mystical faith. Man has proof of the continuity of life not because he has seen or heard or experienced any hint of other worldliness with his limited physical senses, but because he *believes* and *knows*. It is at this very point that Christendom, despite its many denominational expressions, can find a common ground. Those whom the creeds have divided, the hope of the life to come unites.

"For the Christian there is always Christ."

15. Your Will to Believe and You

Recently I interviewed Josef Meier, who plays the part of the *Christus* in the Passion Play. Each summer, thousands of people see him enact this role in the Black Hills of South Dakota and each winter other thousands attend the performance at Lake Wales, Florida.

Mr. Meier, who has enacted the role more than 4,000 times, told me a secret.* He said there was a period in the early history of the play when it seemed that the performances would never "catch on." People apparently were not interested. There was something about the production and the organization that just "didn't click." Often he would meet with his cast and they would discuss the advisability of giving up and disbanding altogether.

* From "The Passion Play Story," by Marcus Bach, published in *Good Business*, April, 1955. Permission granted by *Good Business*, Unity School of Christianity, Lee's Summit, Mo.

What happened? When did a change take place? What "miracle" occurred to turn the project from failure to the phenomenal success it has become? Here is how Mr. Meier explained it:

"One evening when I was playing the part of the *Christus,* as I had done many times before, and on a night when there were very few people in the audience and hope was running low, I came to the lines in the play where Jesus says, 'Why take ye thought for the morrow, O ye of little faith!' I had said these words many, many times. They were part of my performance, a portion of the Master's words to His disciples. On this particular night I heard myself say this line as I had often done, but something happened. For the first time, I asked myself, 'Josef Meier, why don't you have the will to *believe* these words with all your heart? Don't just say them. Believe them!' "

Then he went on to say, "Like a flash it dawned upon me that I had been playing the part of the Christ without actually believing as He believed or living the faith as He lived it. I don't know whether the spectators that night noticed anything new in my interpretation. I don't know whether they sensed that I paused momentarily at this point, but something was happening to me. Belief, trust, conviction came to me and from that moment on a change took place in everything connected with the Passion Play and its future."

180

The Turning Point in Life

That was it. And as he told me this story I could not help but wonder how often we "play the role of the *Christus*," speak His words, hear His words, and even imagine ourselves suffering as He suffered, and never have the will to believe that His words are words of life. Josef Meier in his superb enactment of this delicate and important characterization even hangs upon a literal cross as the *Christus* did, but the "miracle" came only when he suddenly not merely played the part, but *believed* it! That was the turning point. And that is the turning point in every Christian life.

We have been hearers of the word too long and believers and doers of the word too little. America has a greater number of churches, and more beautiful churches, than any other country in the world. It has a greater variety of churches than any other country. More people in America, nearly 60 per cent of our population, are on the church rolls—more than in any other land. Our church music is better and our Sunday Schools are larger, while our contributions to religion are far and away the most generous of any nation of the globe. We are better organized, better staffed, better trained, and better paid than people in religious work anywhere else. But what we desperately need now is the will to live what we profess. And we must begin with a will to

181

believe—a will to believe in the world and the life within, a will to believe in a world and a life around, and a will to believe in a world and a life beyond.

How do we do that? We do it by beginning with ourselves as individuals. You begin with yourself. I begin with myself. And when we have persuaded enough individuals to enter into this will to believe, each for himself, then and only then will religion become the power and the glory it is intended to be.

Let Us Write Our Will to Believe as We Look Toward a New Tomorrow!

I remember author Thomas Sugrue. Perhaps you remember how he answered the question about Christian fellowship and Christian union. When he was asked, "How and through whom will this come about?" he answered, "Through the Catholics and Protestants who look to the Sermon on the Mount for their ideal, and who try—falling a thousand times a day—to live up to that ideal.

"They are the men and women—church members of all sects and of all religions—who believe in fulfilling the law of God in its spiritual and not in its physical sense. . . . They are the salt of the earth, the salt which has not lost its savor. There are a few of them in each community in America. But together they form the leaven which keeps the loaf of Christianity raised, and which prevents religion from descending to the level of a farce. These people, wherever two or three of them are gathered—and where, therefore, He is in their midst —can do something about sectarianism." *

And, we might add, almost *every* problem which has been talked about and argued about and discussed for generation upon generation has never, honestly and co-operatively, been acted upon with a sincere will to believe that it can be solved.

Faith Is the Answer

Writing in "The Literary Spotlight," a Chicago book review column, of Ethel Waters and her impressive book, *His Eye Is on the Sparrow*, Fanny Butcher said, "I went last night to a banquet at which Ethel Waters was being honored. I went expecting it would be just another one of those things. Then Miss Waters got up to speak. When I heard her, I realized that to her God is no vague philosophical concept. He is in the air she breathes and in the ground upon which she walks. She knows as few human beings know that underneath her life are the everlasting arms. How she was able to maintain this faith during the trying periods of her life

---

* Thomas Sugrue, *A Catholic Speaks His Mind on America's Religious Conflict* (New York: Harper & Bros., 1952), pp. 60-61.

183

is little less than a miracle, but now, even though her hair is grey, she still erupts with laughter as spontaneously as Yellowstone Park erupts with geysers!"

How was she able to "maintain this faith?" By a will to believe in the world and the life within . . . and around . . . and beyond.

Here Is the Challenge

To do good in a world that is evil, and to be honest at a time when dishonesty may seem to be expedient; to hold to the hope of peace in the midst of strife; to love and not hate; to build and not destroy; to be true to one's highest ideals at a time when ideals may not seem to matter much any more; to have the faith that in all, and around all, and above all, is God who is just and true—that is exercising the will to believe in our time.